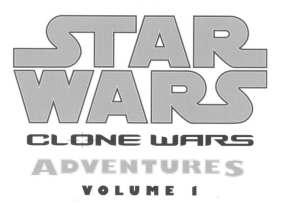

STAR WARS

CLONE WARS

ADVENTURES

VOLUME 1

designer
Darin Fabrick

associate editor
Jeremy Barlow

editor
Randy Stradley

publisher
Mike Richardson

special thanks to Sue Rostoni and Amy Gary
at Lucas Licensing

talk about this book online at: *www.darkhorse.com/community/boards*

The events in this story take place approximately
five months after the Battle of Geonosis.

Dark Horse Books
A division of Dark Horse Comics, Inc.
10956 S.E. Main Street
Milwaukie, OR 97222

First edition: July 2004
ISBN-10: 1-59307-243-0
ISBN-13: 978-1-59307-243-8

7 9 10 8

STAR WARS®

CLONE WARS
ADVENTURES
VOLUME 1

"BLIND FORCE"
script **Haden Blackman**
art and colors **Ben Caldwell**

"HEAVY METAL JEDI"
script **Haden Blackman**
art **The Fillbach Brothers**
colors **Sno Cone Studios, Ltd.**

"FIERCE CURRENTS"
script **Haden Blackman**
art **The Fillbach Brothers**
colors **Sno Cone Studios, Ltd.**

lettering
Michael David Thomas

cover
Ben Caldwell

Dark Horse Books™

DURING THE HEIGHT OF THE CLONE WARS...

MASTER... I THINK I'VE FIXED THE HALO LAMP.

GOOD WORK.

NOW WE'LL BE ABLE TO SEE WHAT WE'RE DOING OUT HERE...

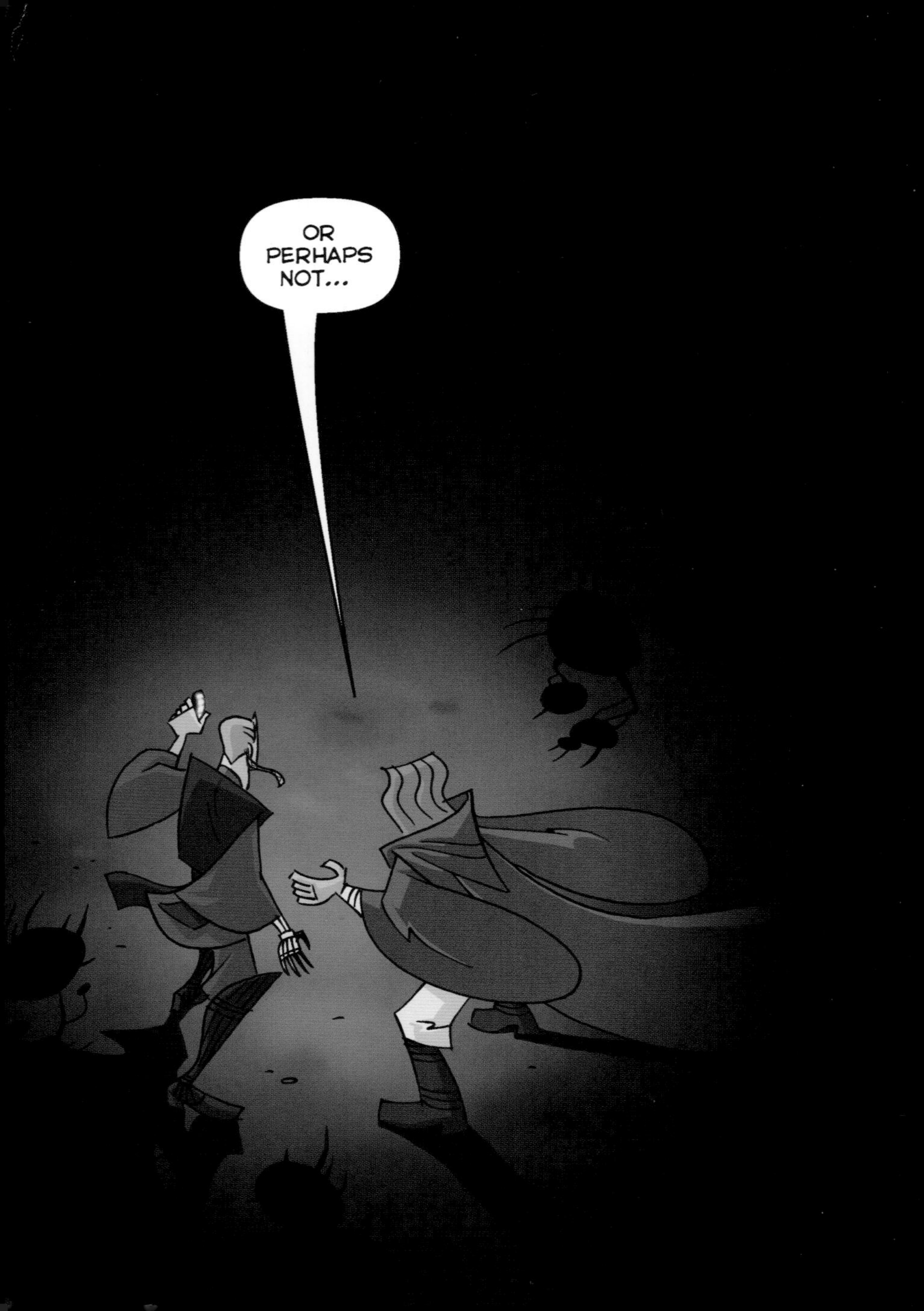
OR PERHAPS NOT...

OBI-WAN KENOBI AND
ANAKIN SKYWALKER IN:

A CLONE WARS ADVENTURE

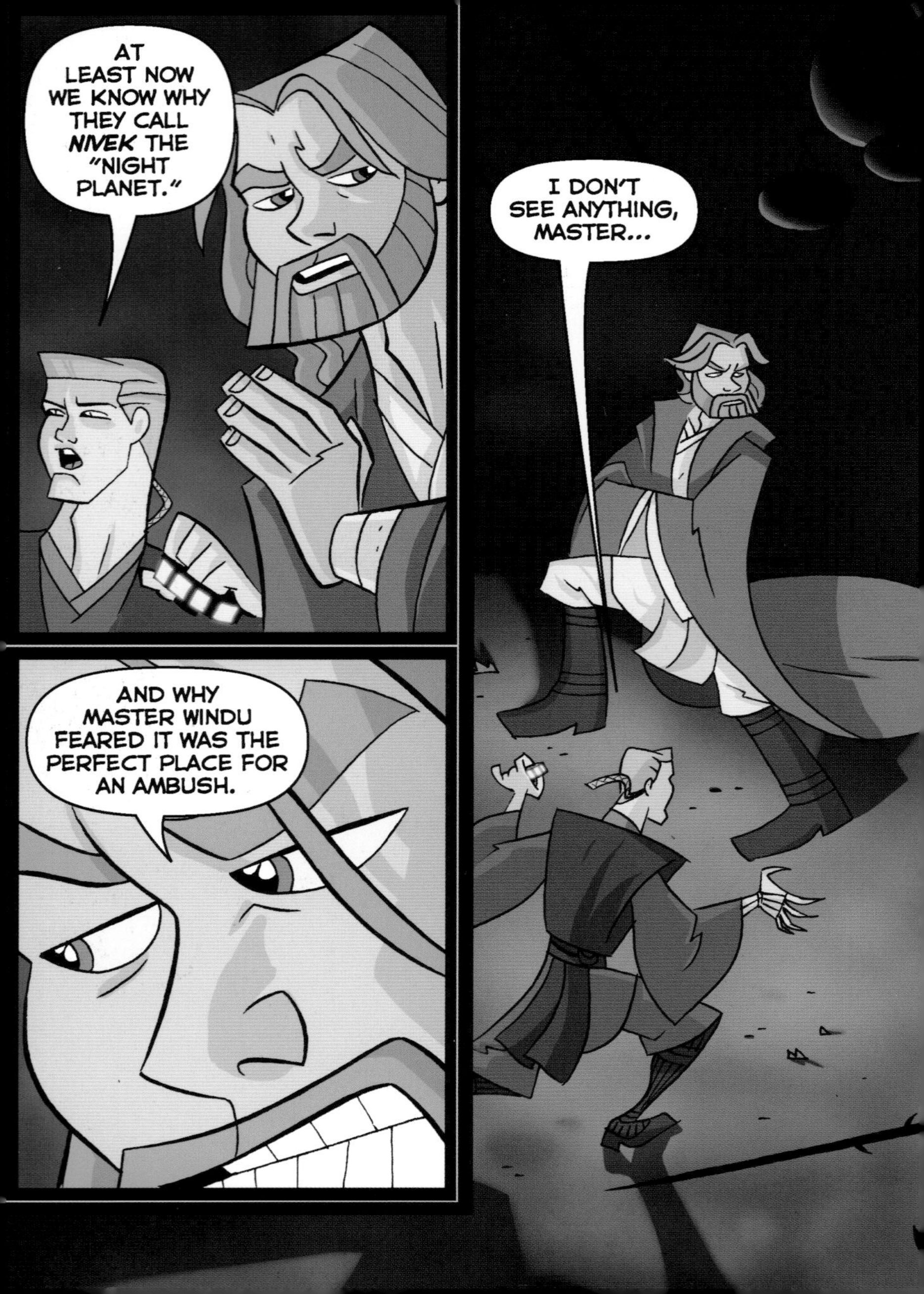
AT LEAST NOW WE KNOW WHY THEY CALL *NIVEK* THE "NIGHT PLANET."
AND WHY MASTER WINDU FEARED IT WAS THE PERFECT PLACE FOR AN AMBUSH.
I DON'T SEE ANYTHING, MASTER...

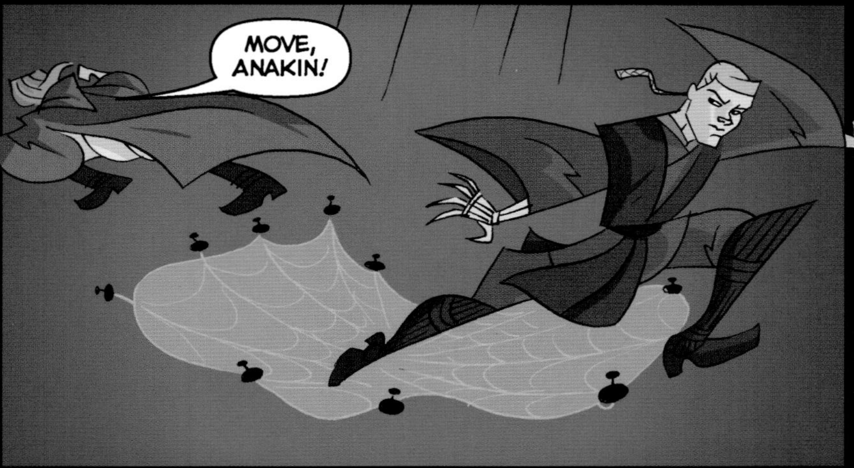
MOVE, ANAKIN!

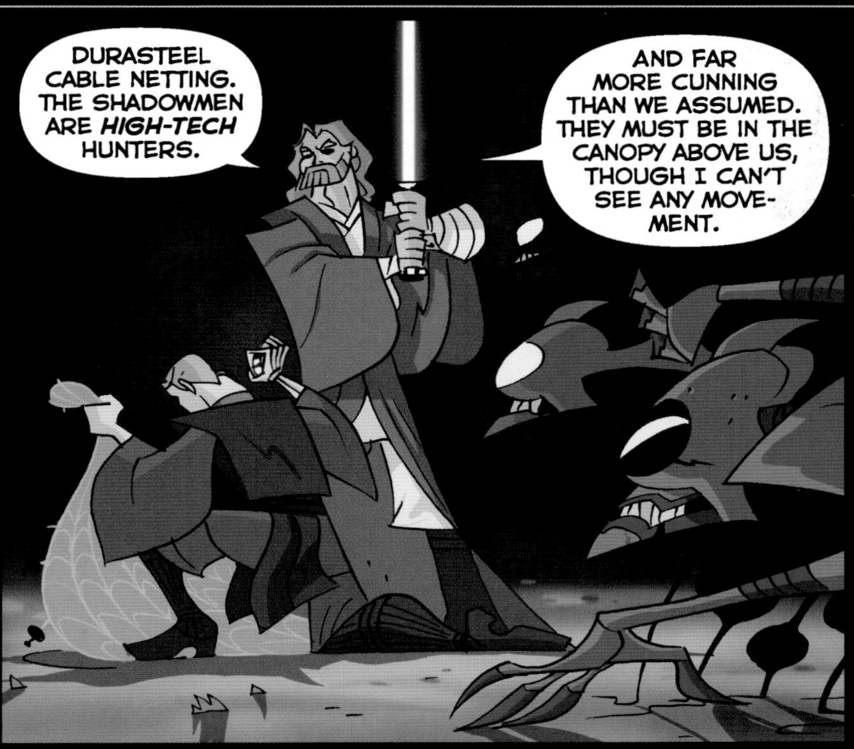
DURASTEEL CABLE NETTING. THE SHADOWMEN ARE *HIGH-TECH* HUNTERS.
AND FAR MORE CUNNING THAN WE ASSUMED. THEY MUST BE IN THE CANOPY ABOVE US, THOUGH I CAN'T SEE ANY MOVE-MENT.

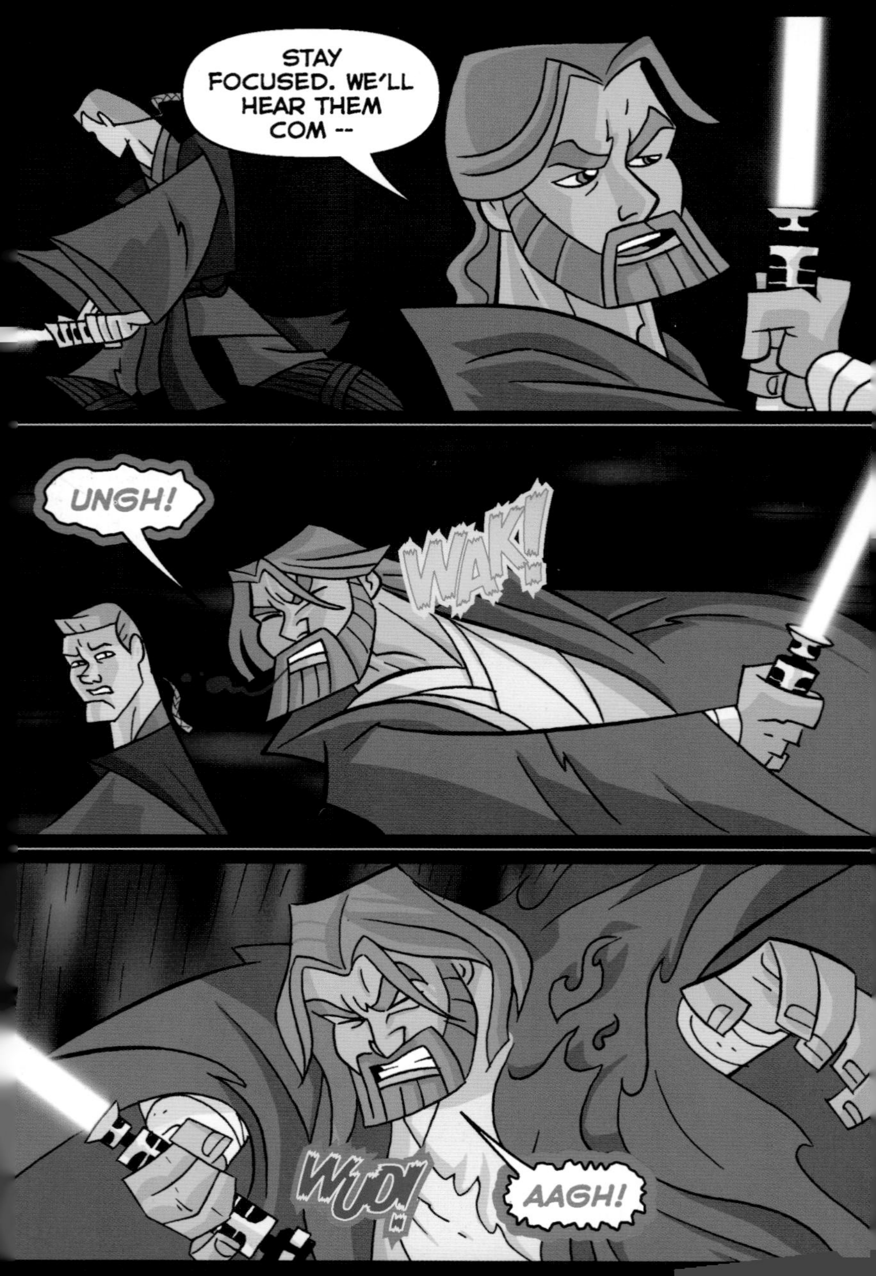
STAY FOCUSED. WE'LL HEAR THEM COM --
UNGH!
WAK!
WUD!
AAGH!

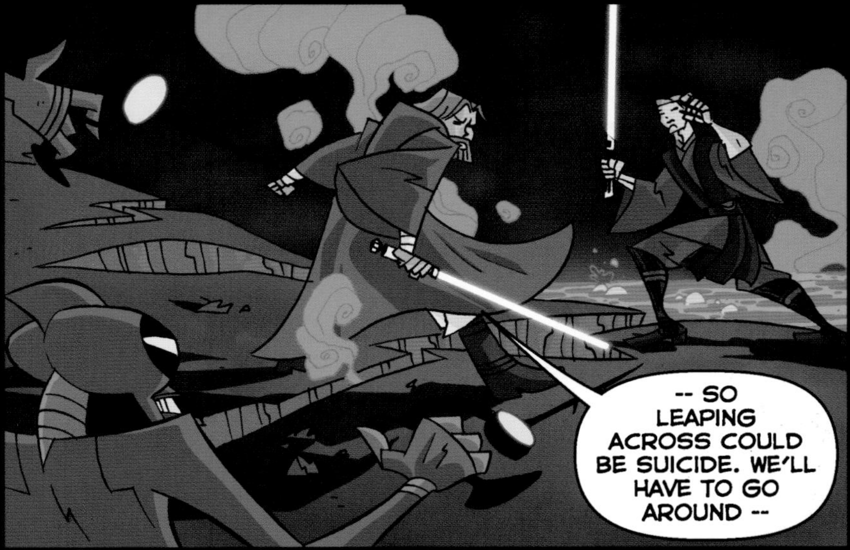
-- SO LEAPING ACROSS COULD BE SUICIDE. WE'LL HAVE TO GO AROUND --
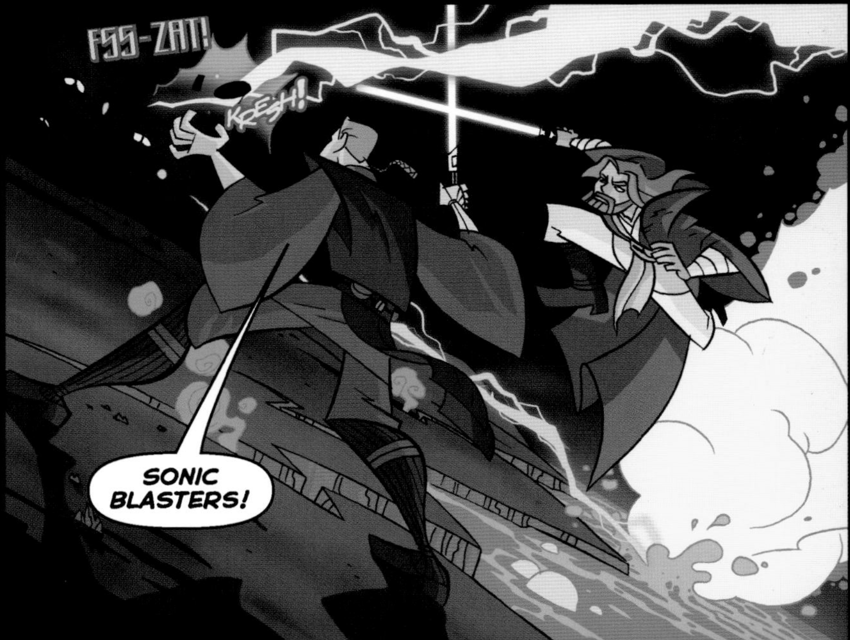
FSS-ZAT!
KRESH!
SONIC BLASTERS!

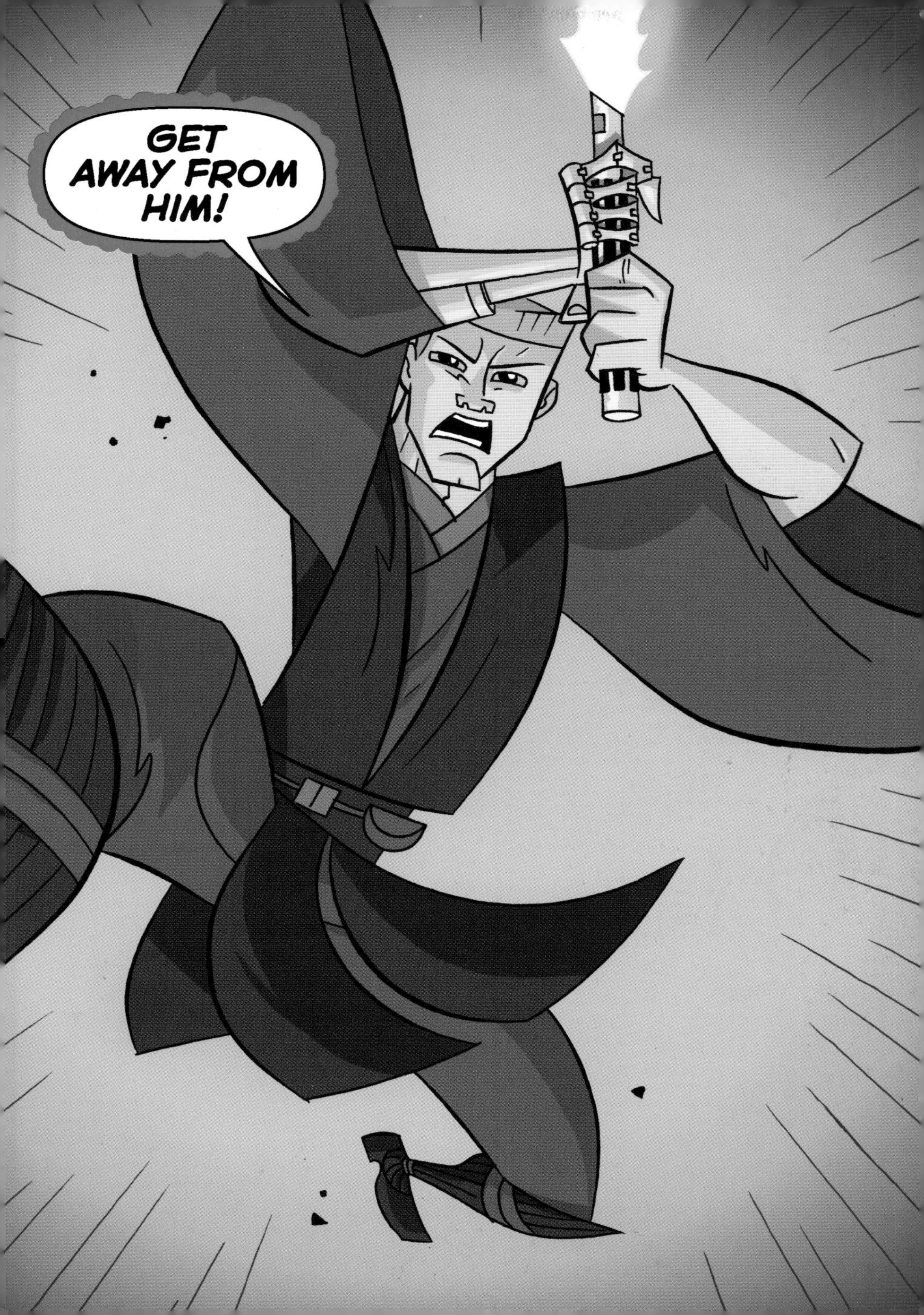
GET AWAY FROM HIM!

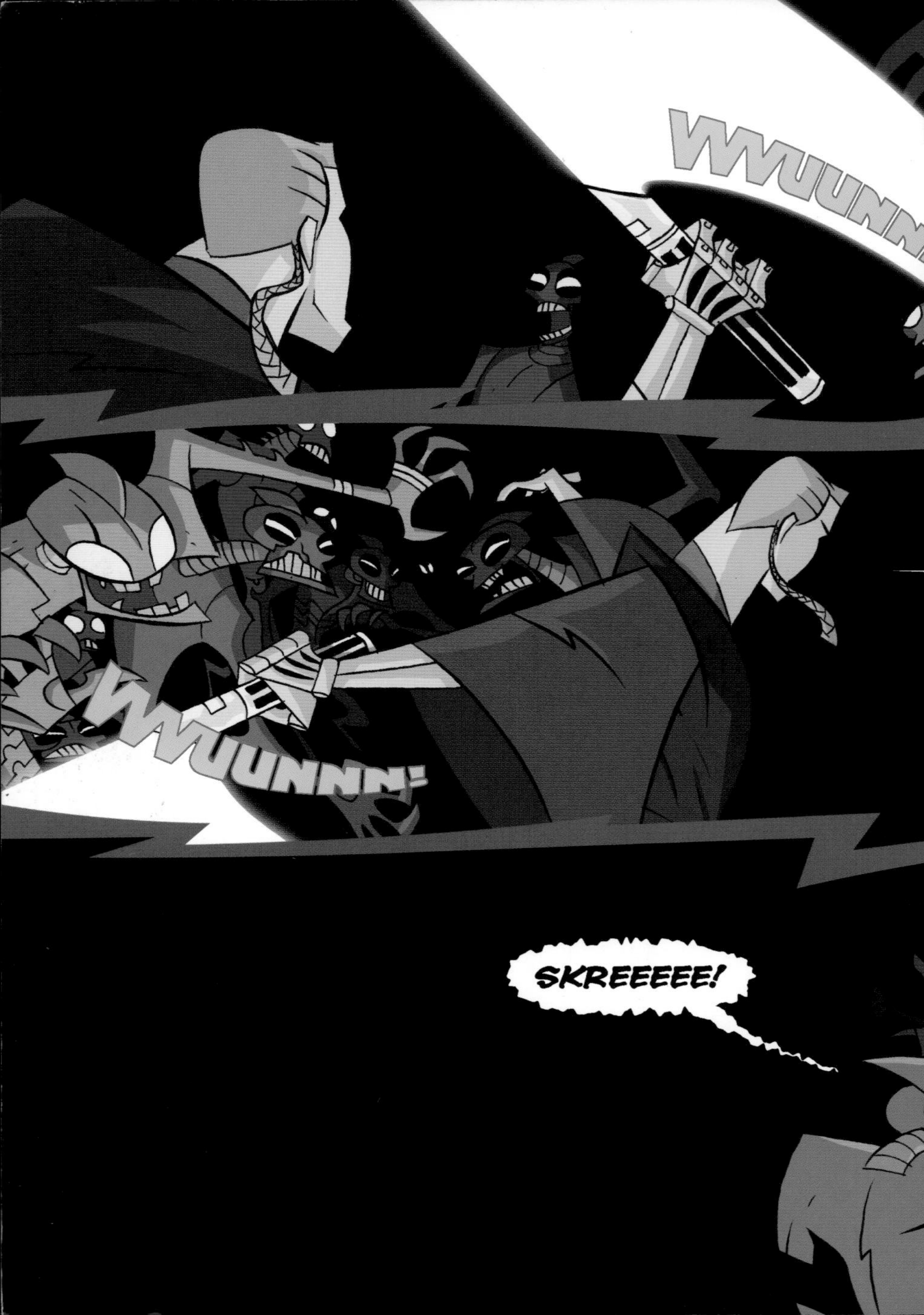
WWUUNNN!
WWUUNNN!
SKREEEEEE!

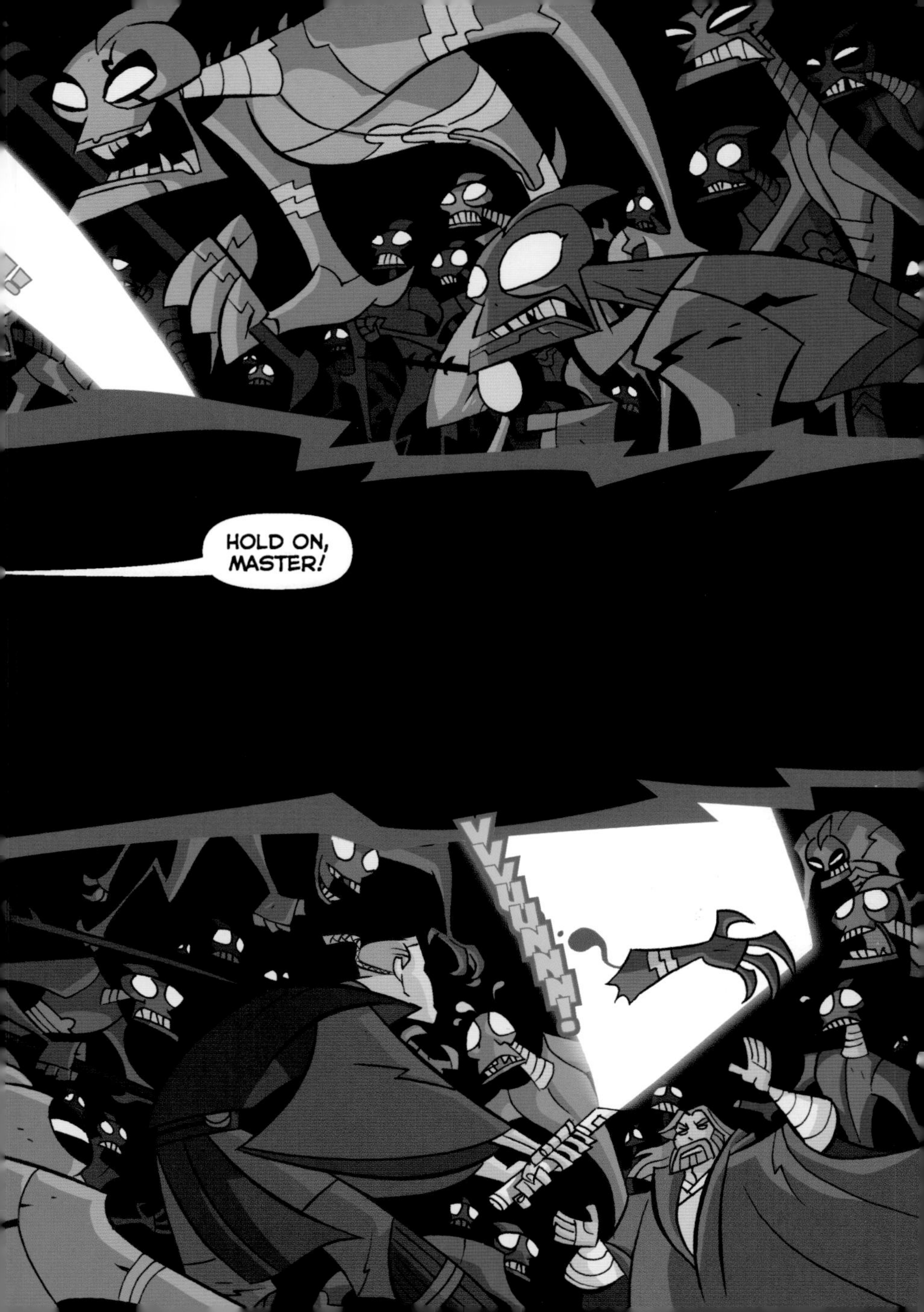
HOLD ON, MASTER!
VVVUUNNN!

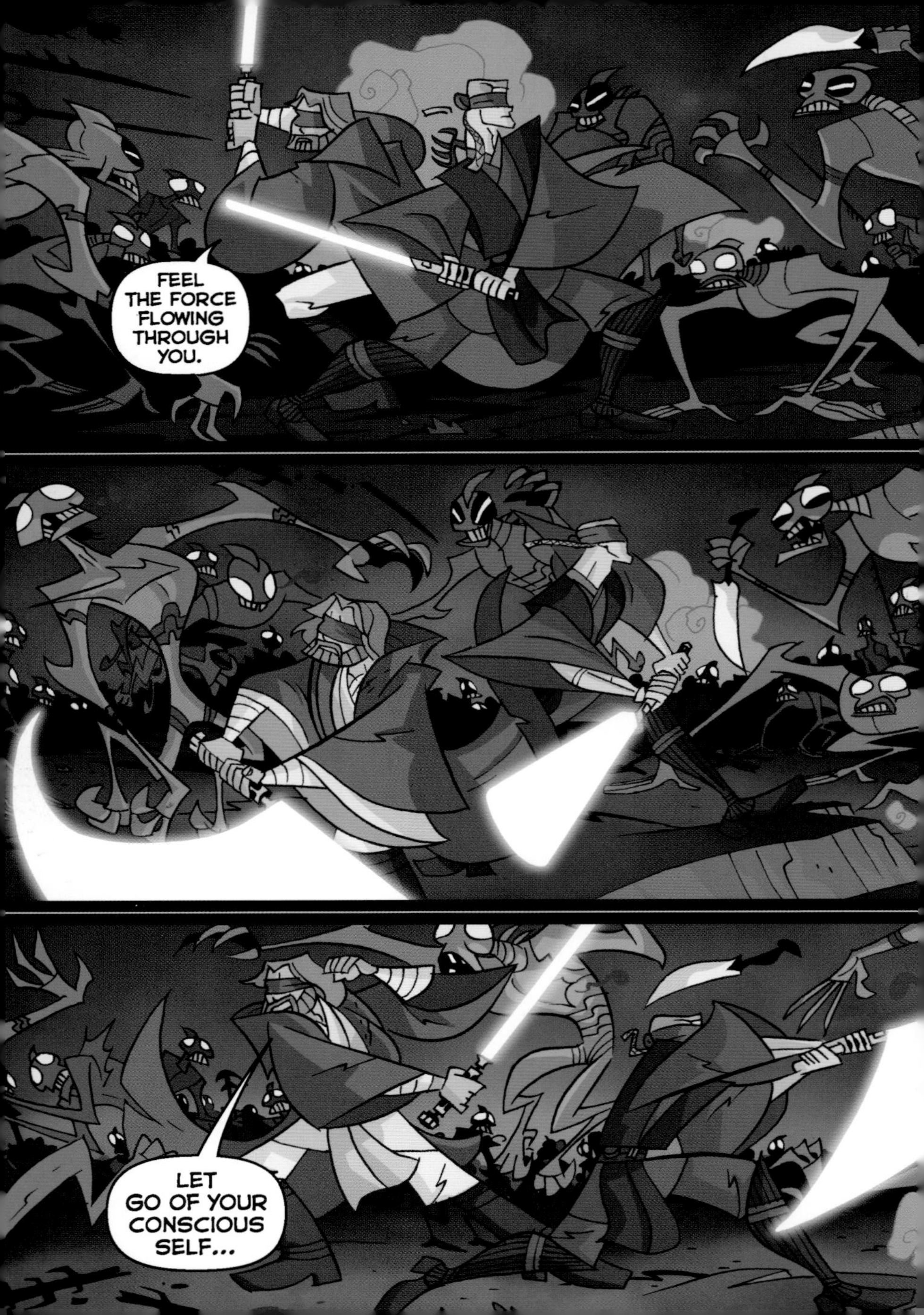
FEEL THE FORCE FLOWING THROUGH YOU.
LET GO OF YOUR CONSCIOUS SELF...

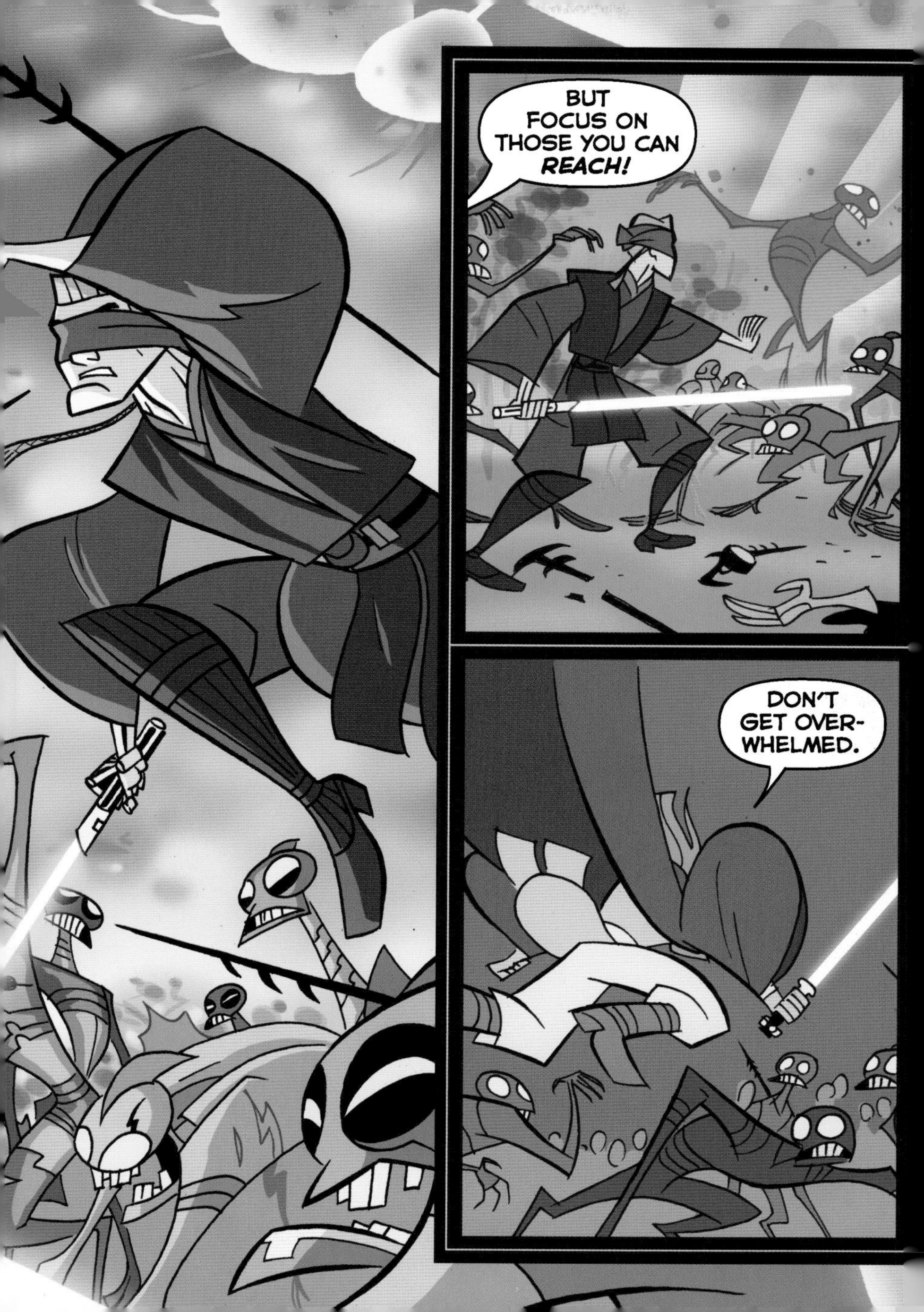
BUT FOCUS ON THOSE YOU CAN *REACH!*
DON'T GET OVER-WHELMED.

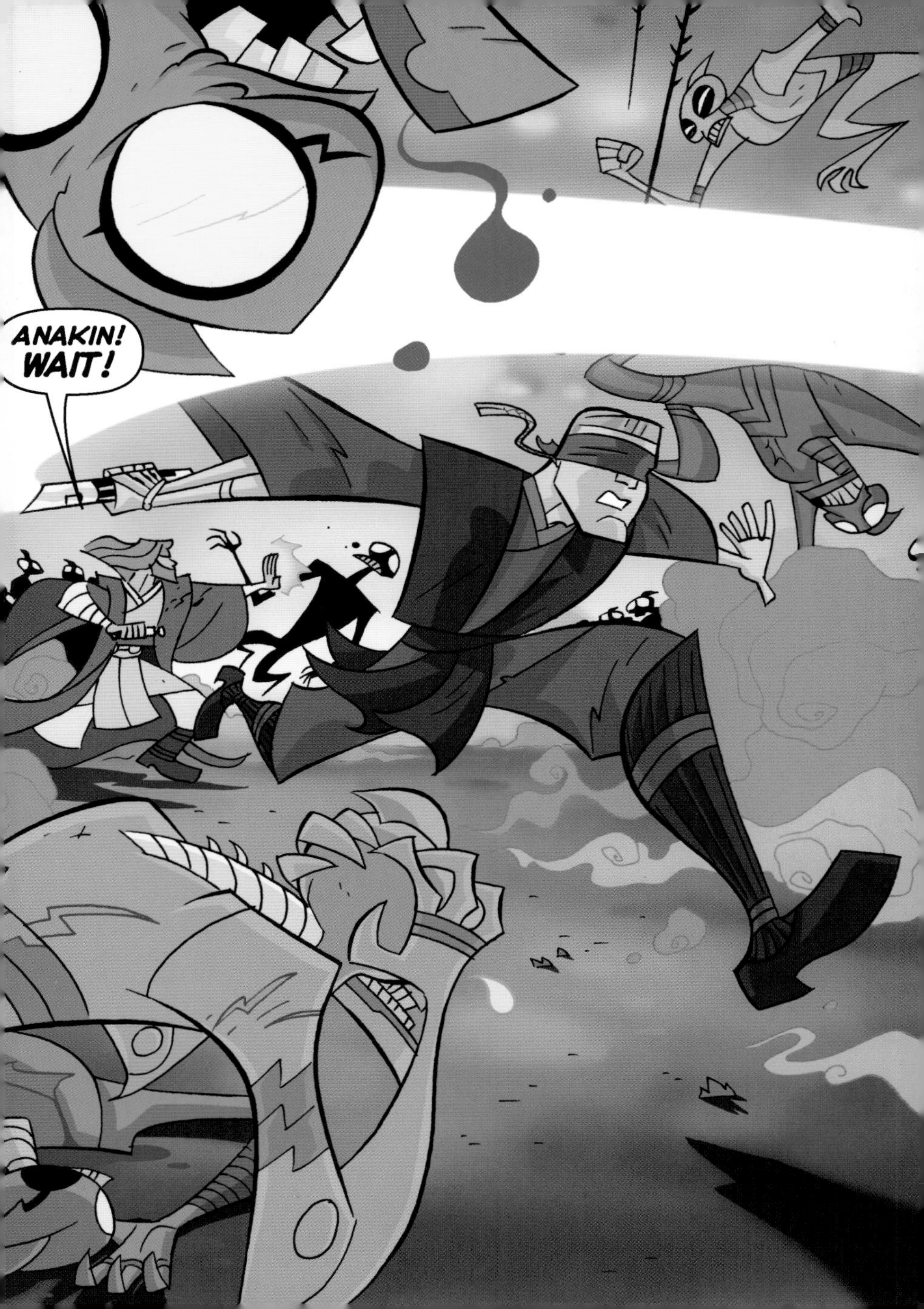
ANAKIN! WAIT!

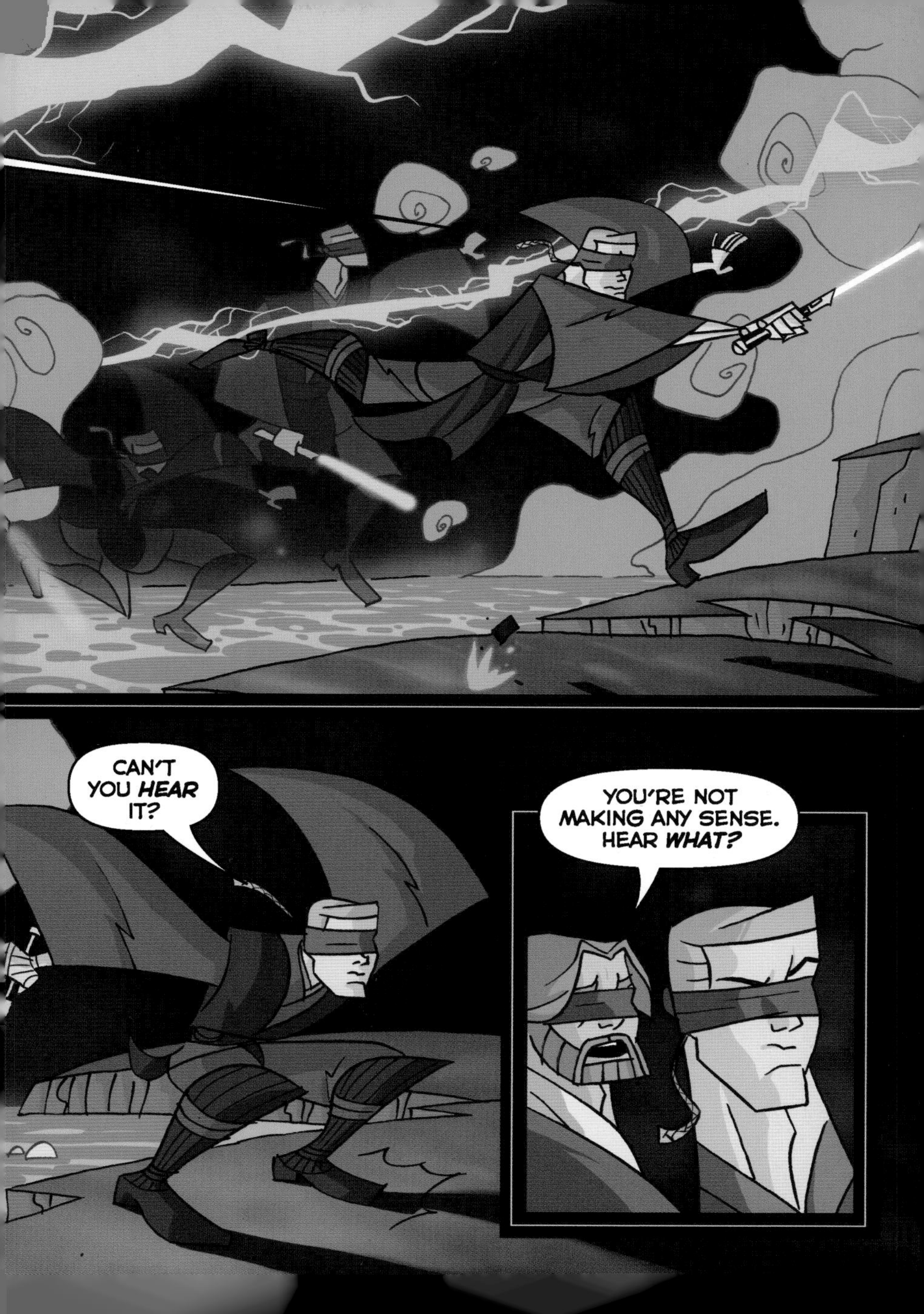
CAN'T YOU *HEAR* IT?
YOU'RE NOT MAKING ANY SENSE. HEAR *WHAT?*

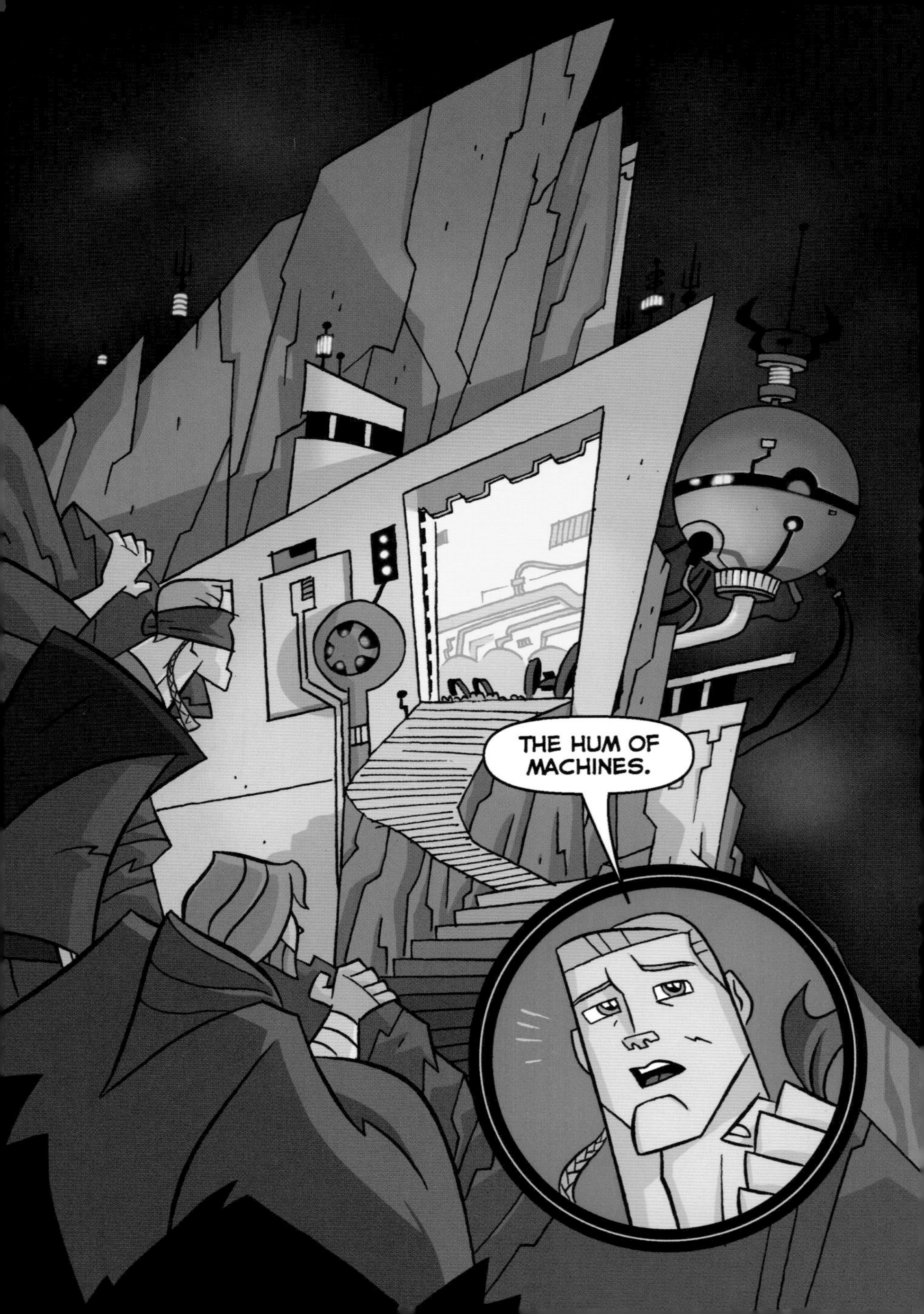
THE HUM OF MACHINES.

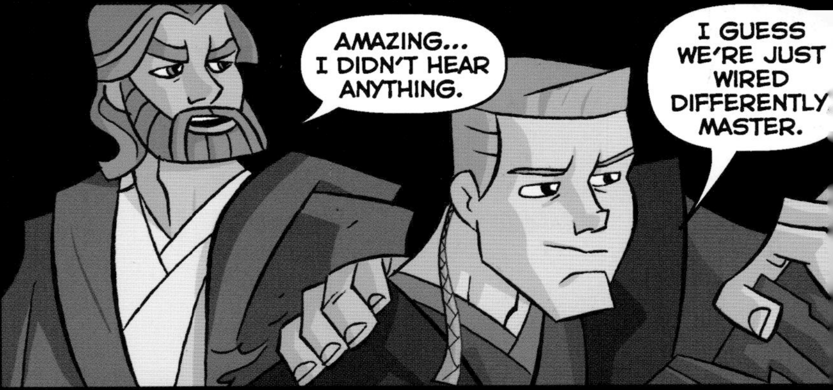
AMAZING... I DIDN'T HEAR ANYTHING.
I GUESS WE'RE JUST WIRED DIFFERENTLY MASTER.
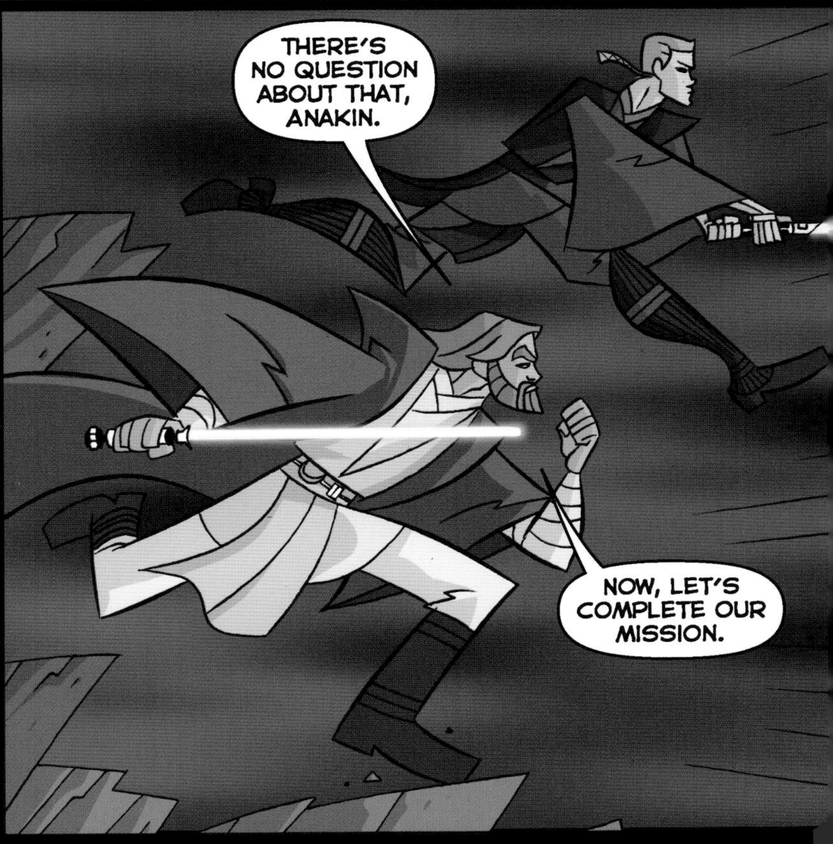
THERE'S NO QUESTION ABOUT THAT, ANAKIN.
NOW, LET'S COMPLETE OUR MISSION.

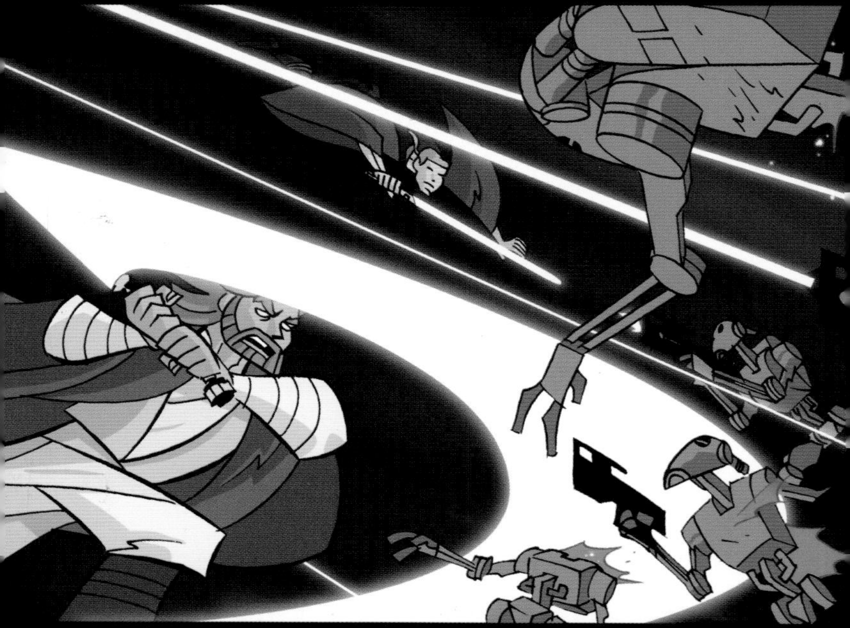
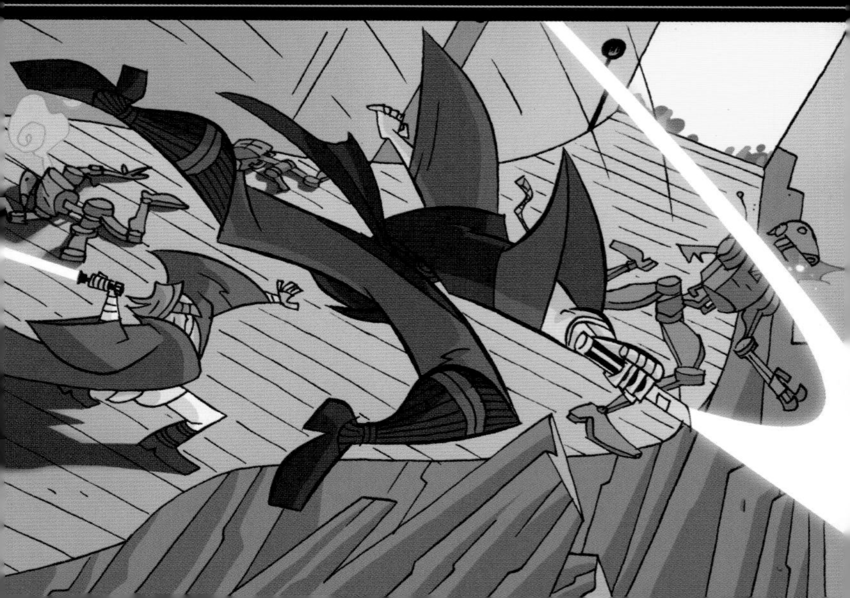

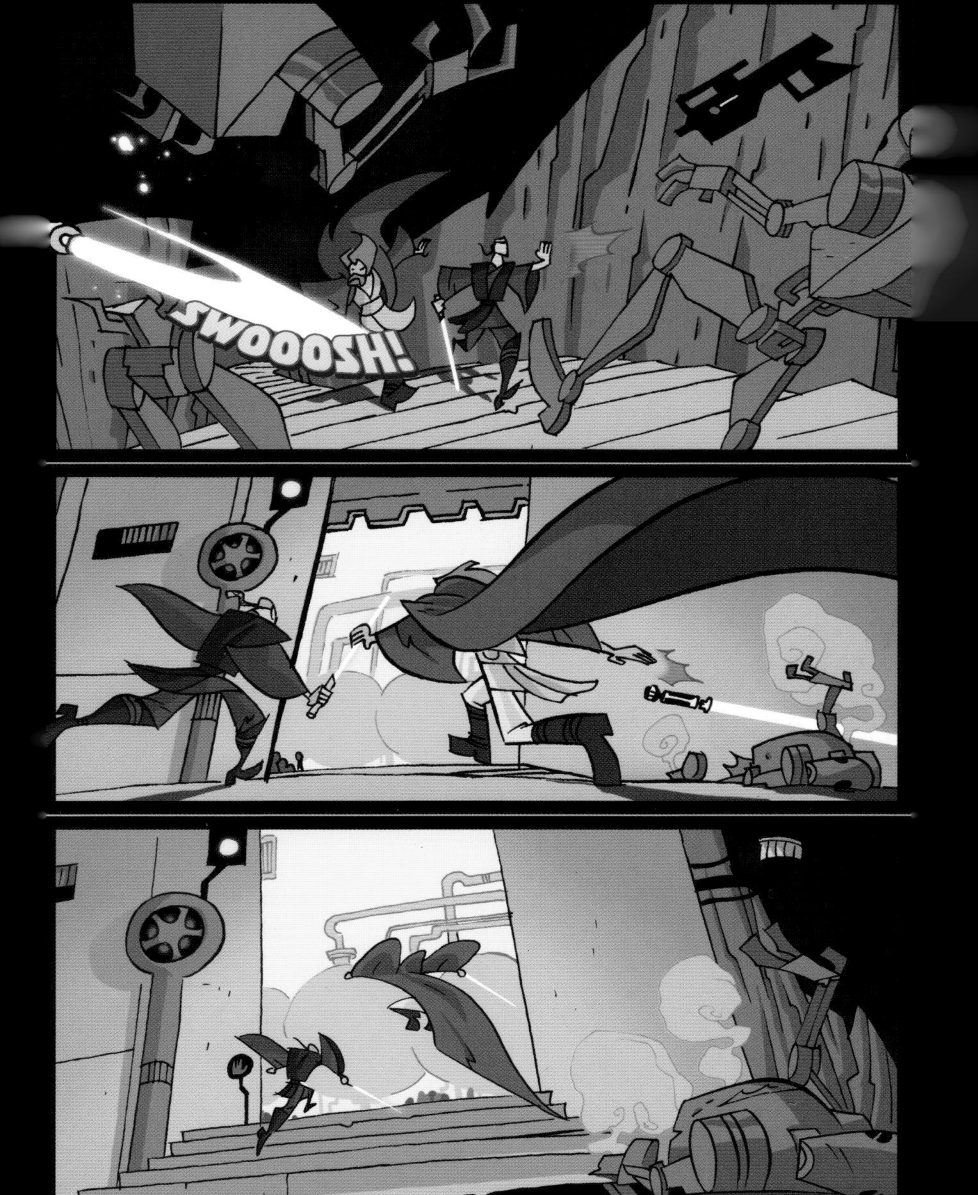
SWOOOSH!

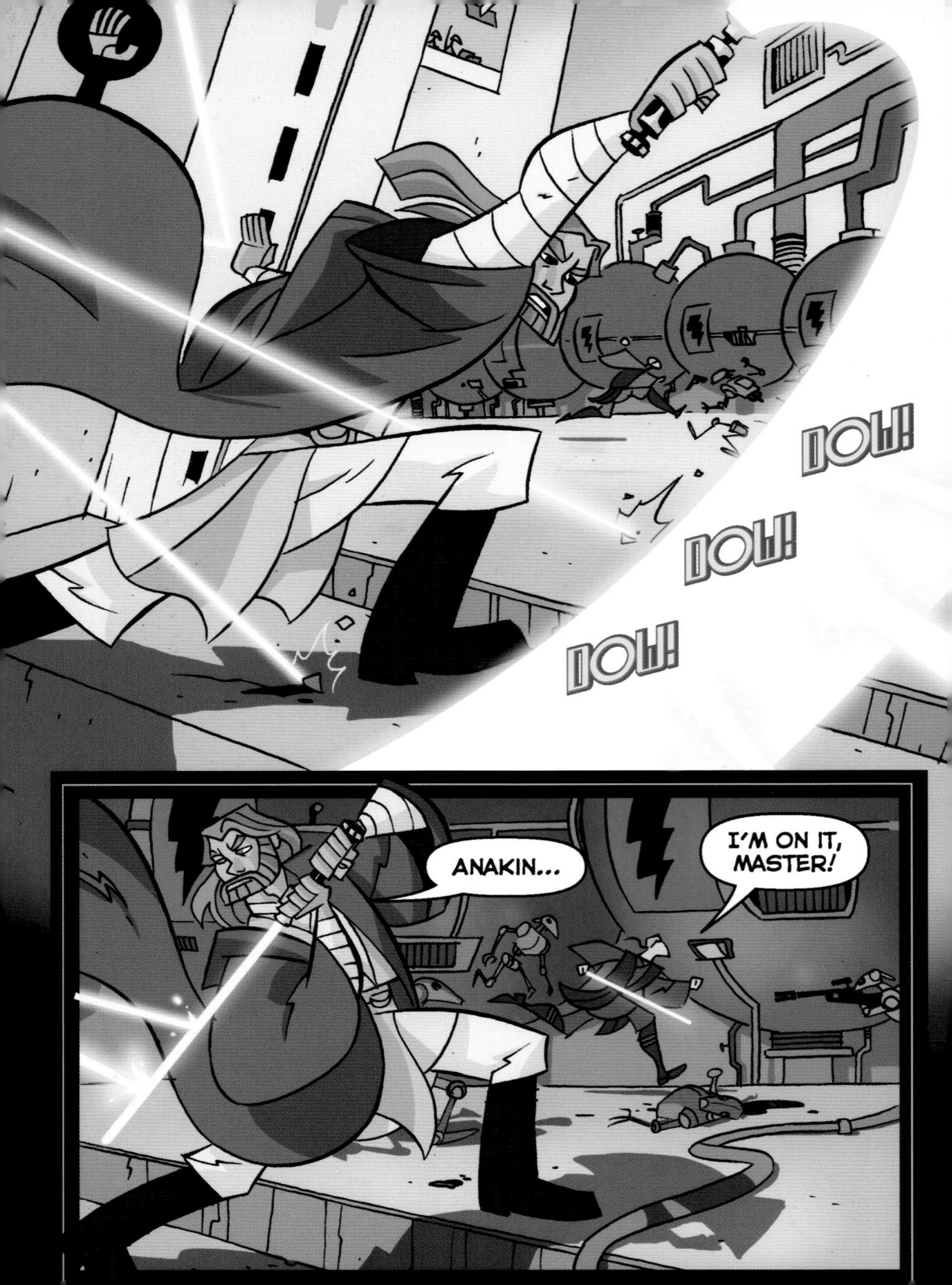
DOW!
DOW!
DOW!
ANAKIN...
I'M ON IT, MASTER!

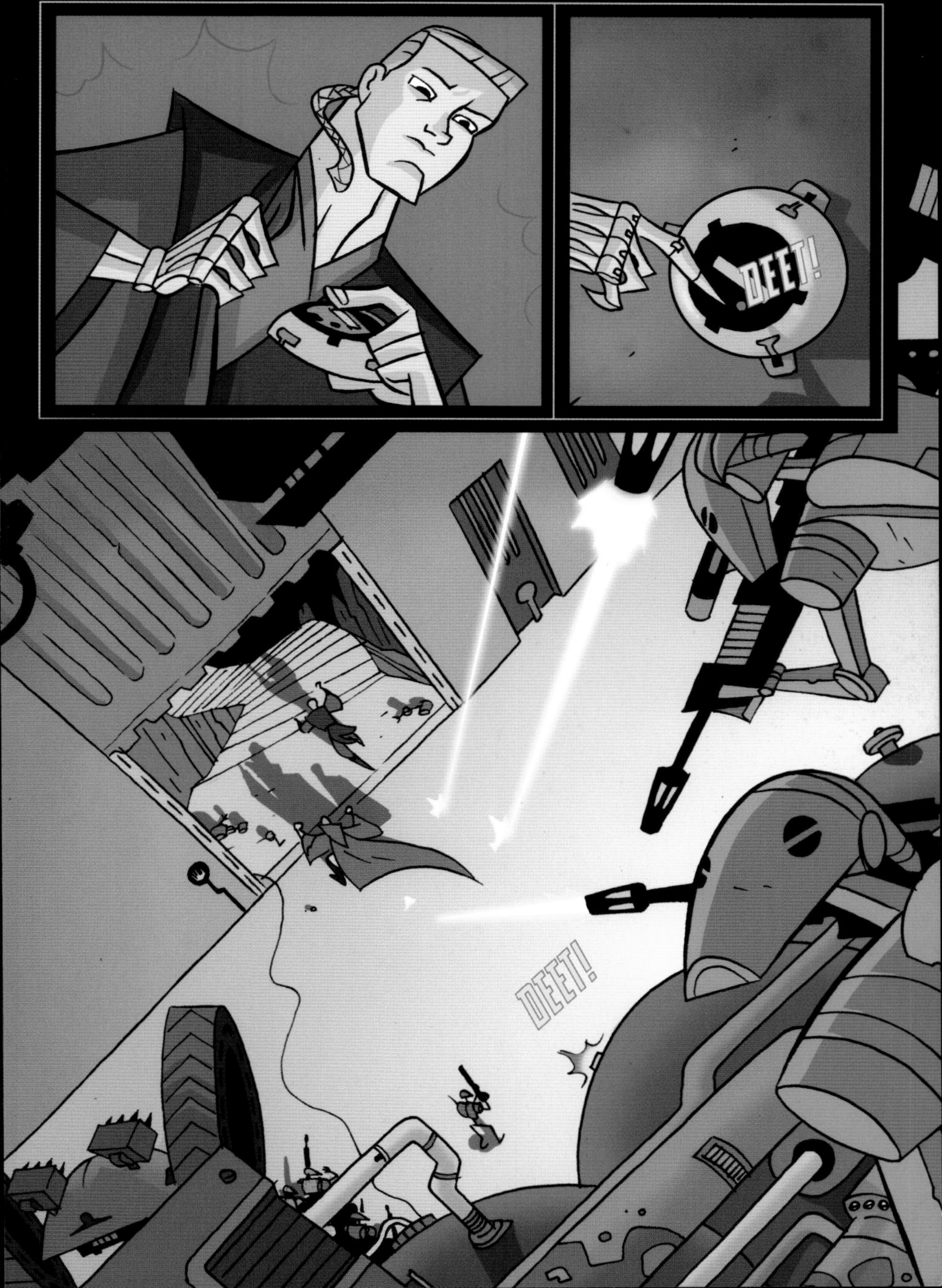
DEET!
DEET!

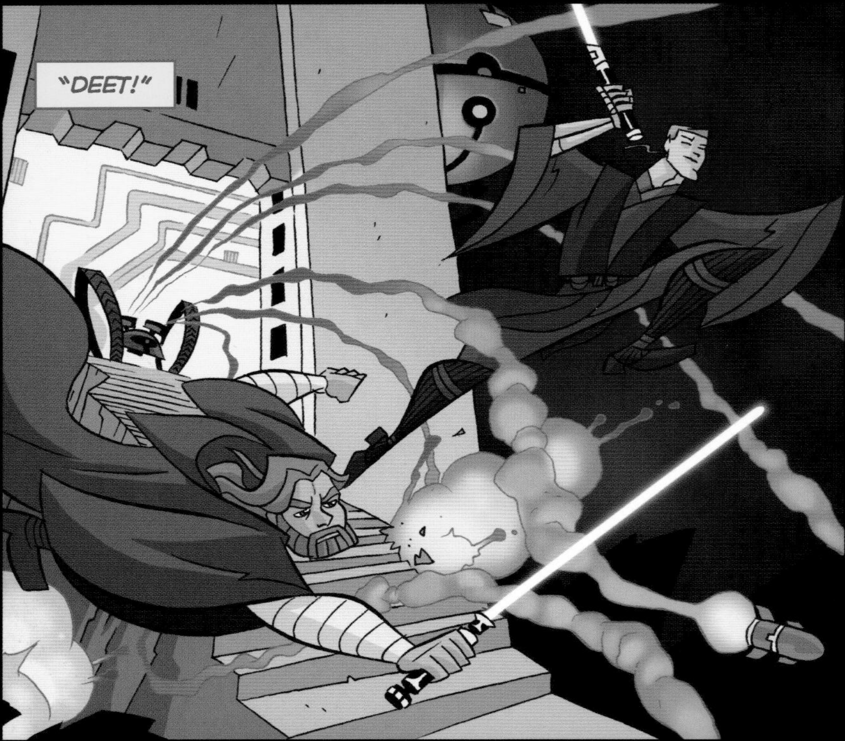
"DEET!"

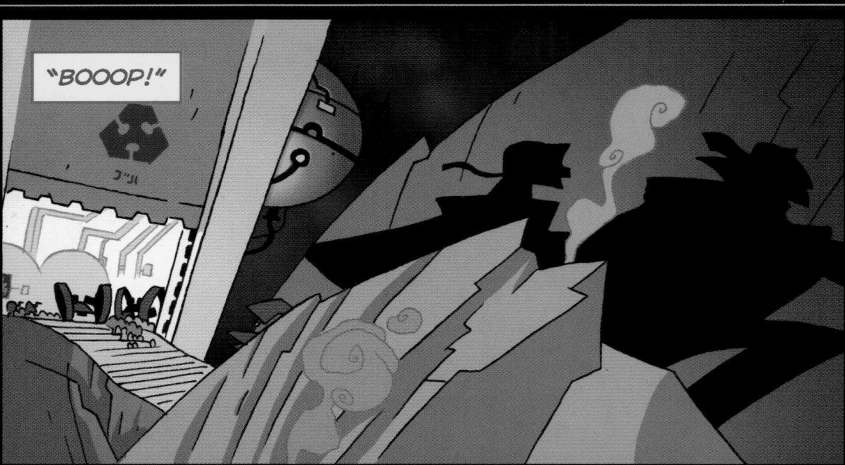
"BOOOP!"

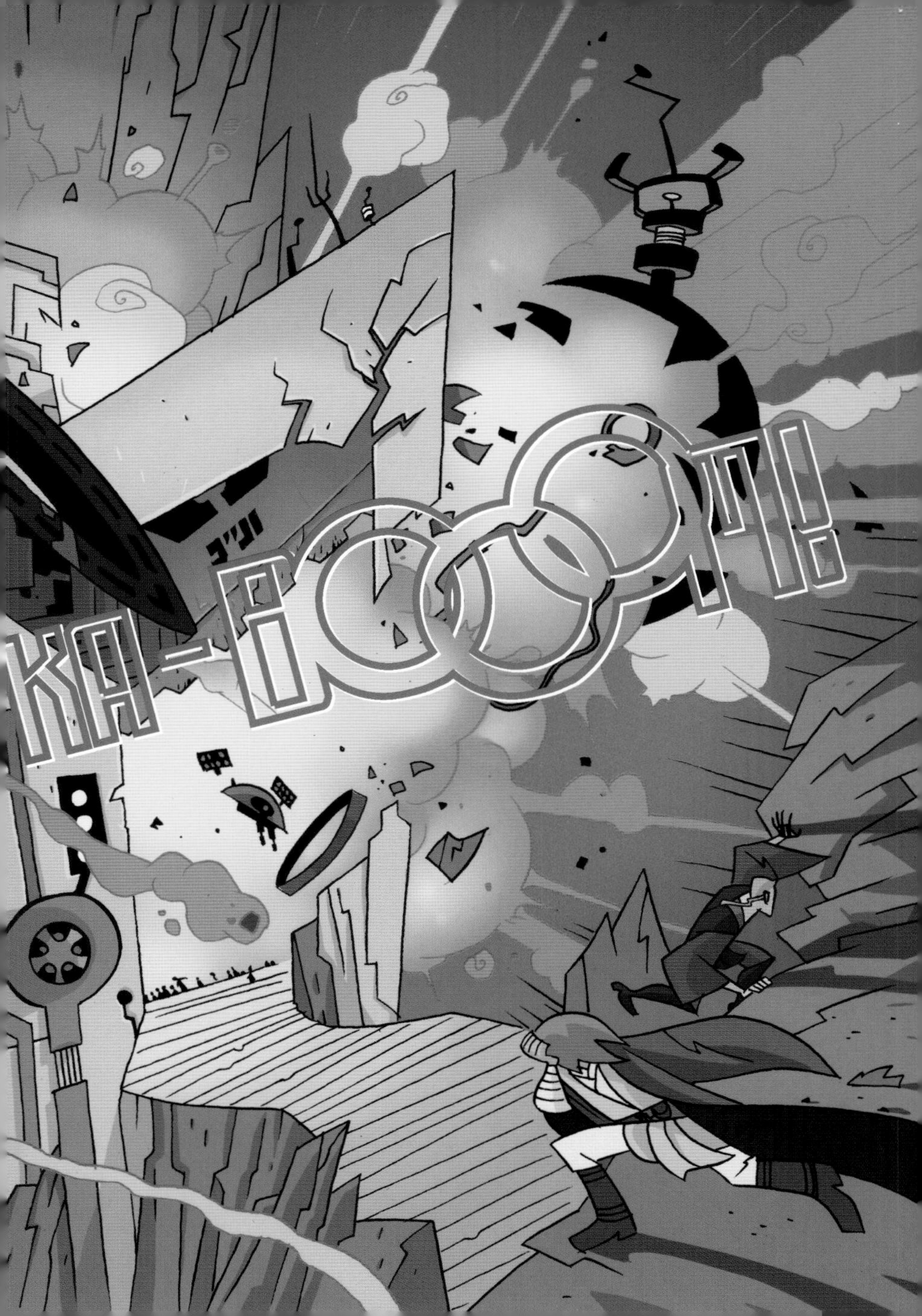
KA-BOOOM!

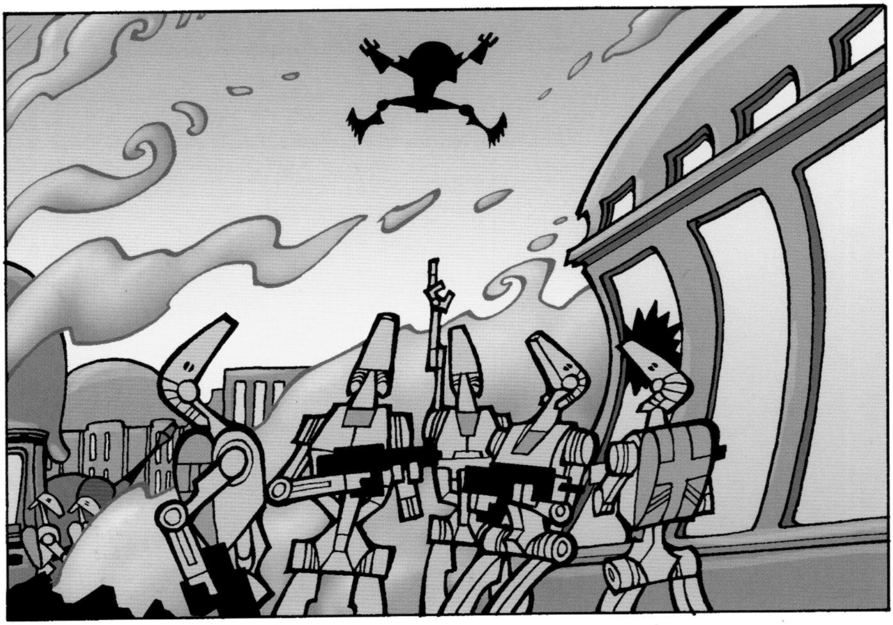

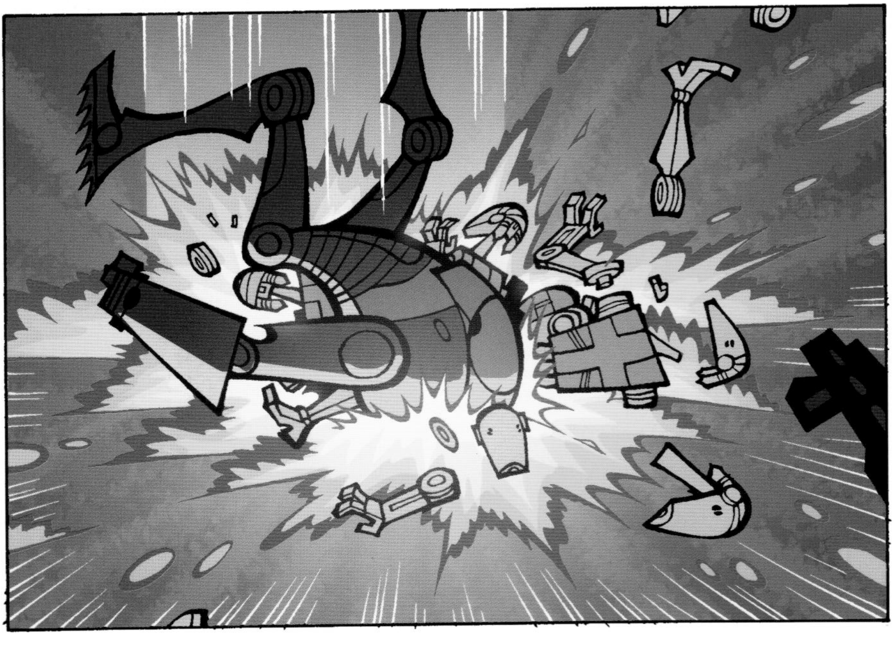

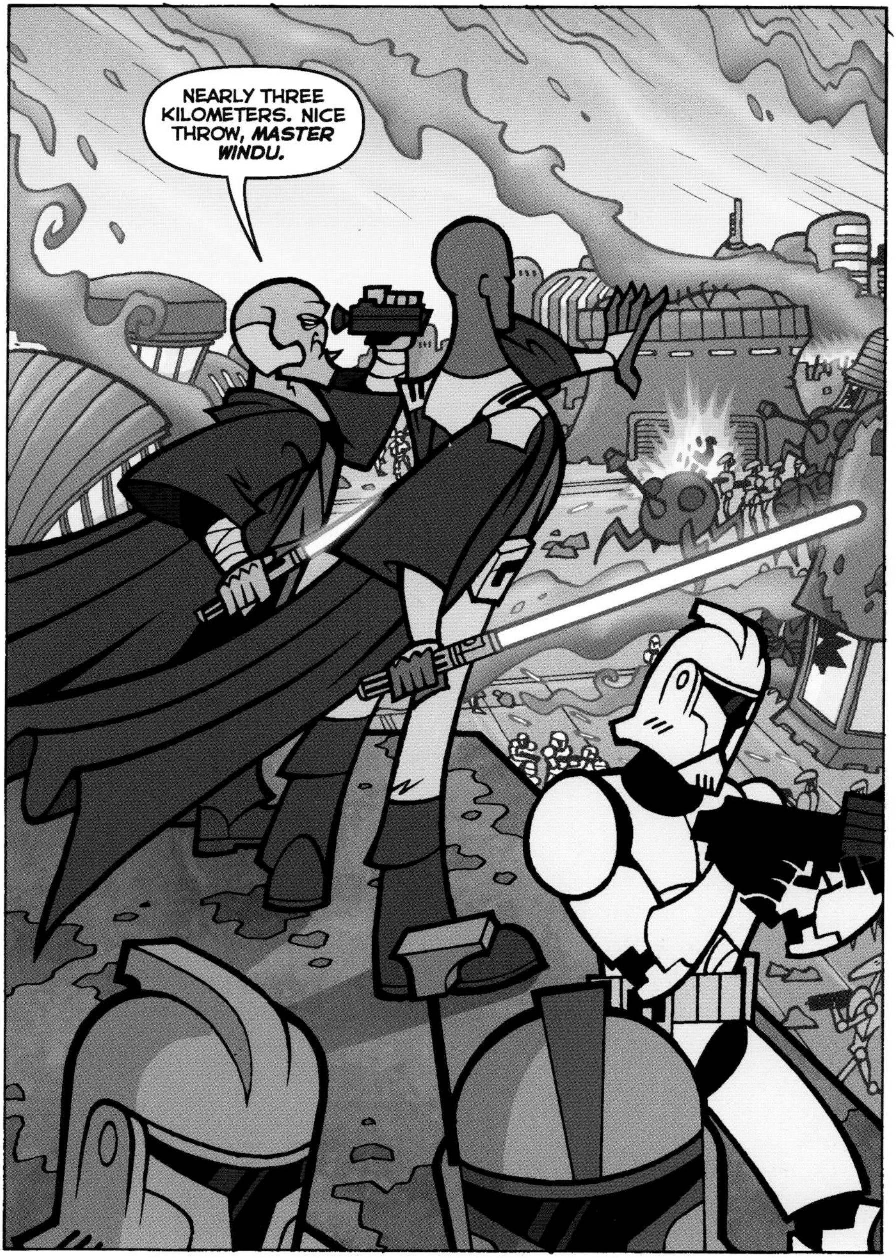
NEARLY THREE KILOMETERS. NICE THROW, *MASTER WINDU.*

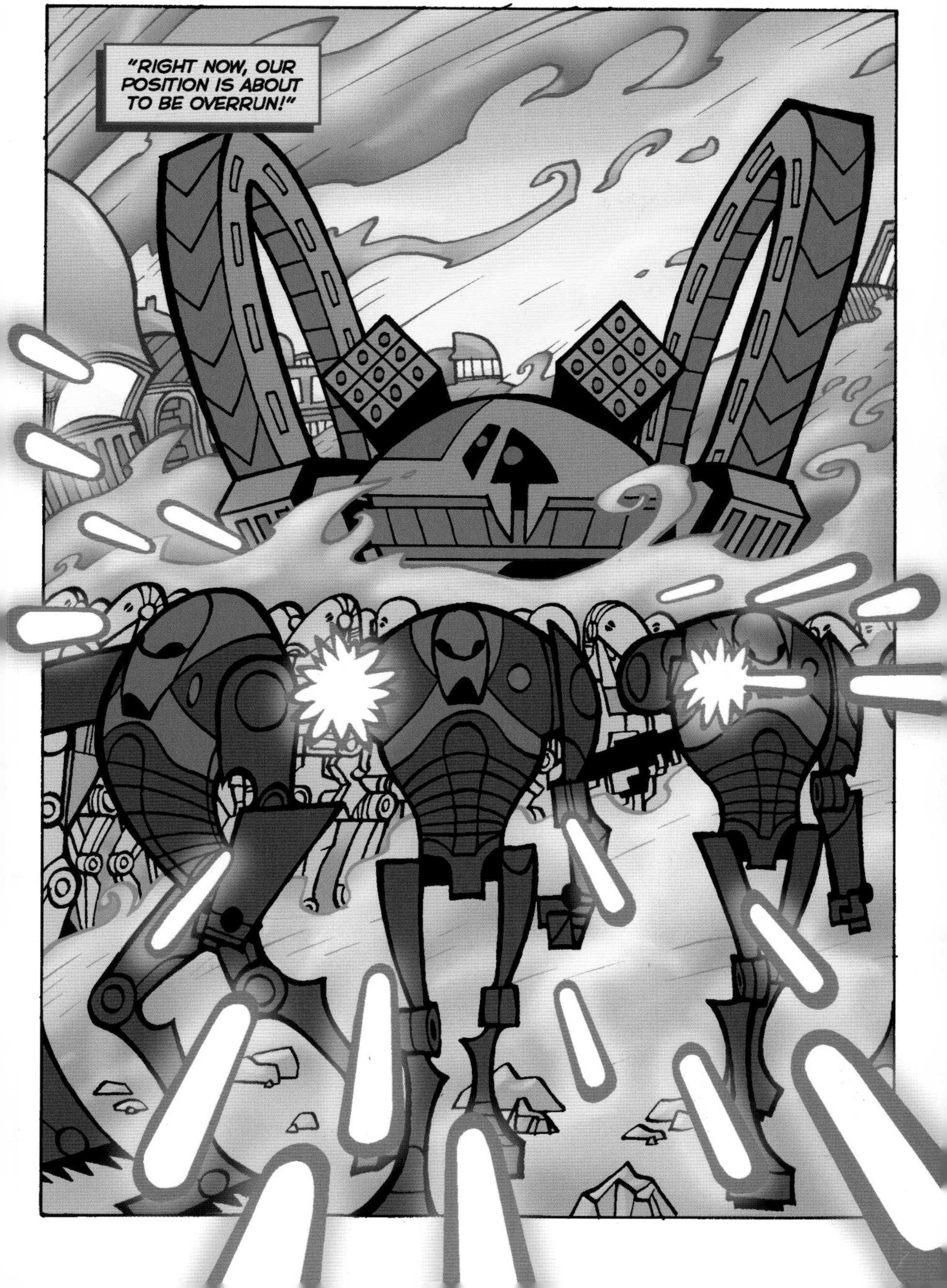
"RIGHT NOW, OUR POSITION IS ABOUT TO BE OVERRUN!"

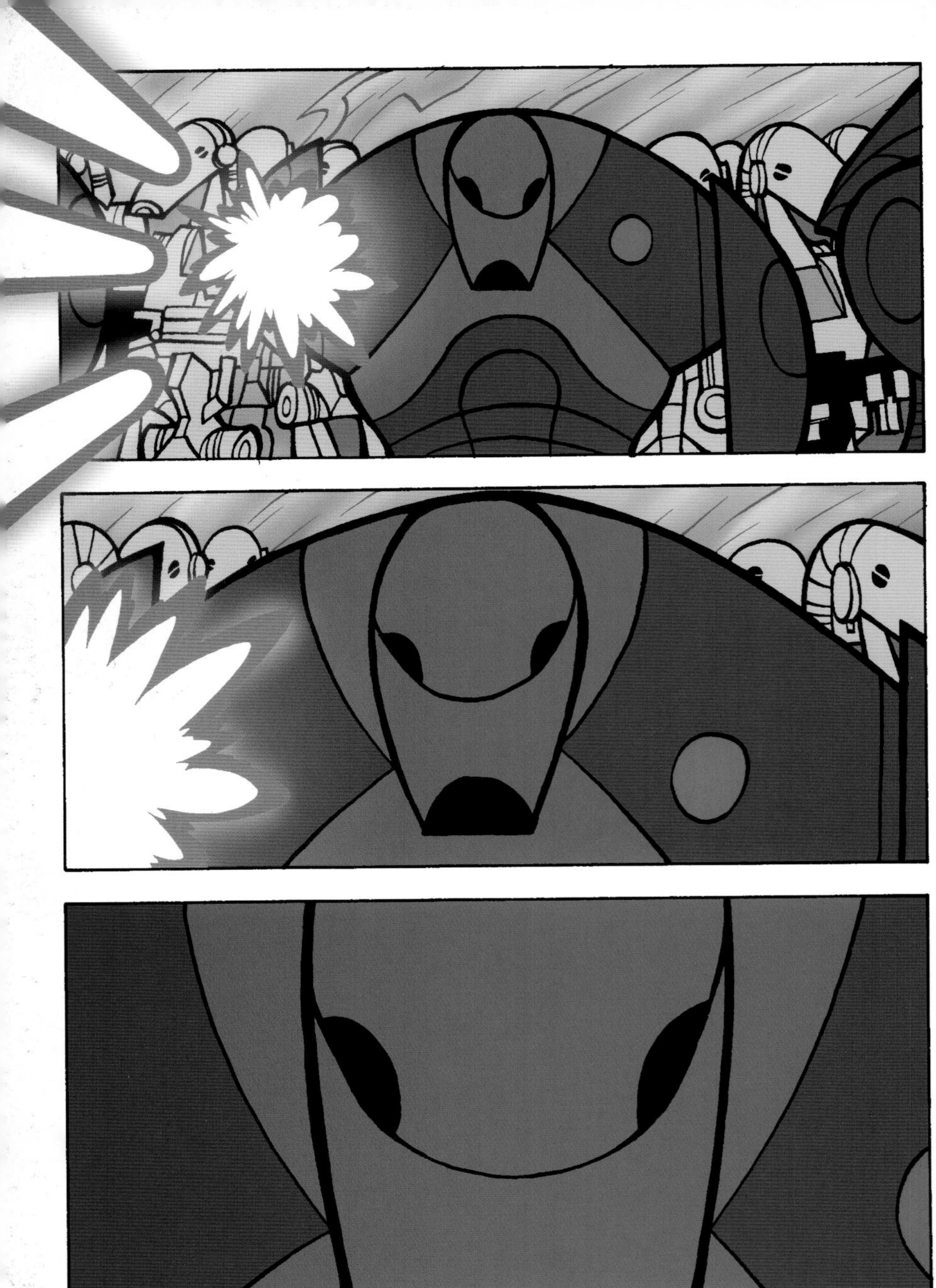

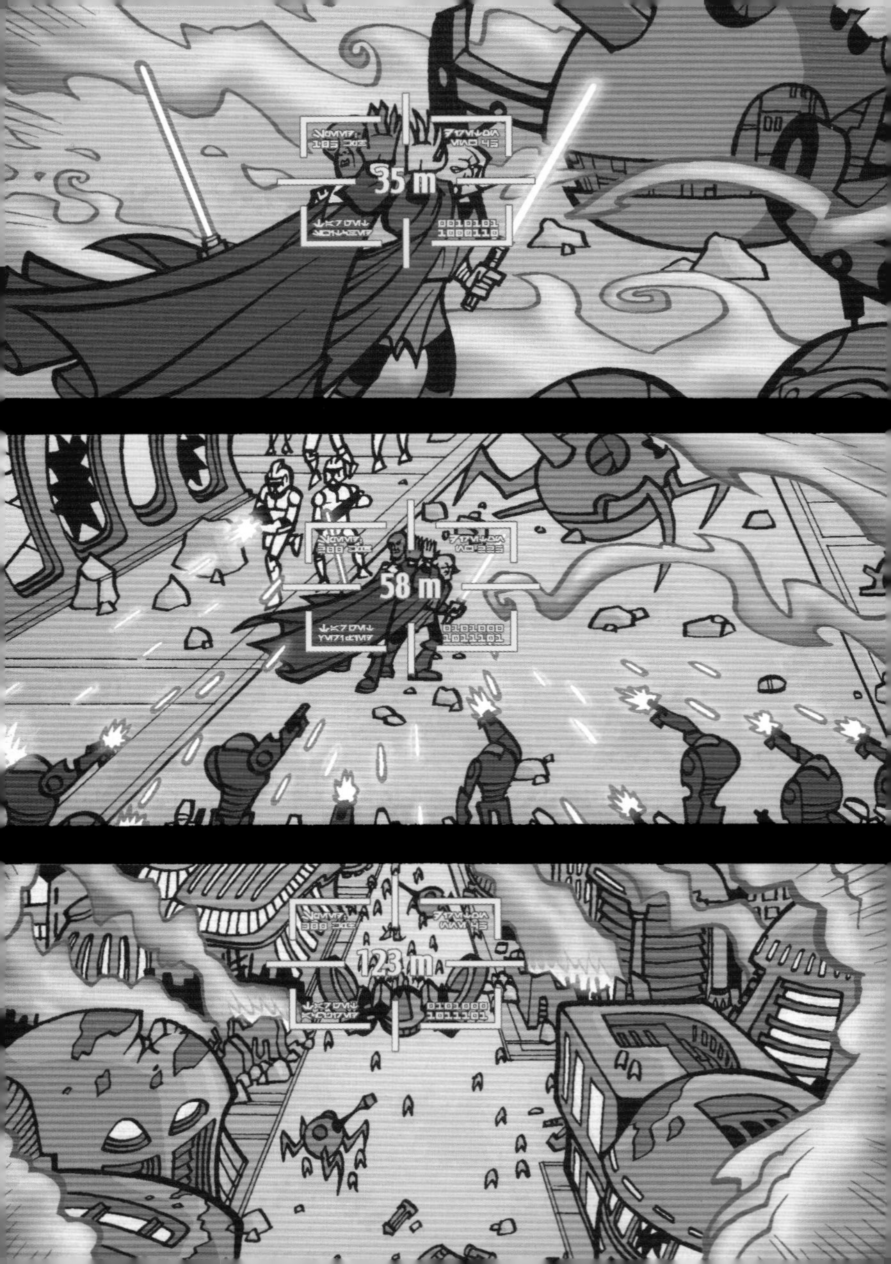
35 m
0010101
1000110
58 m
0101000
1011101
123 m
0101000
1011101

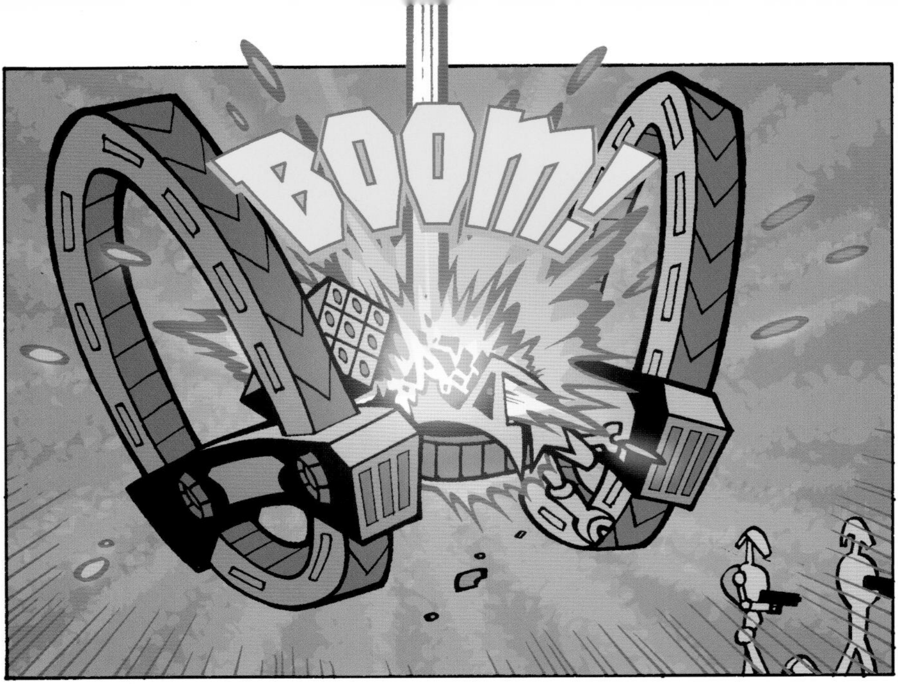
BOOM!

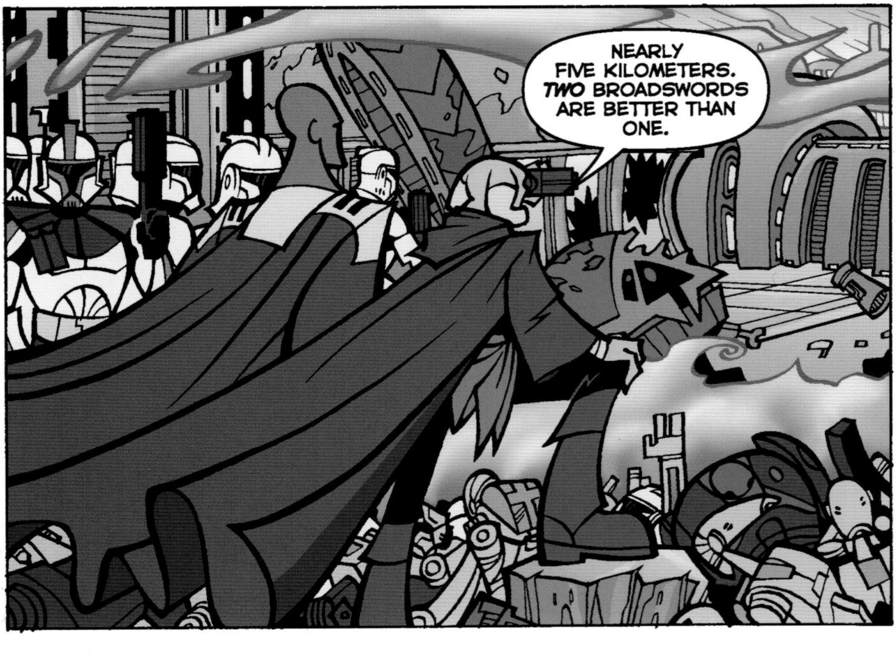
NEARLY FIVE KILOMETERS. *TWO* BROADSWORDS ARE BETTER THAN ONE.

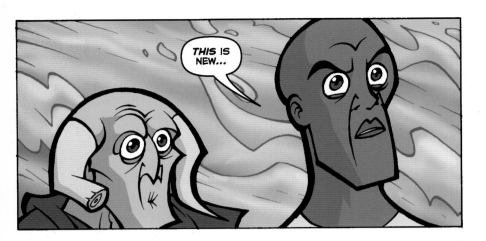

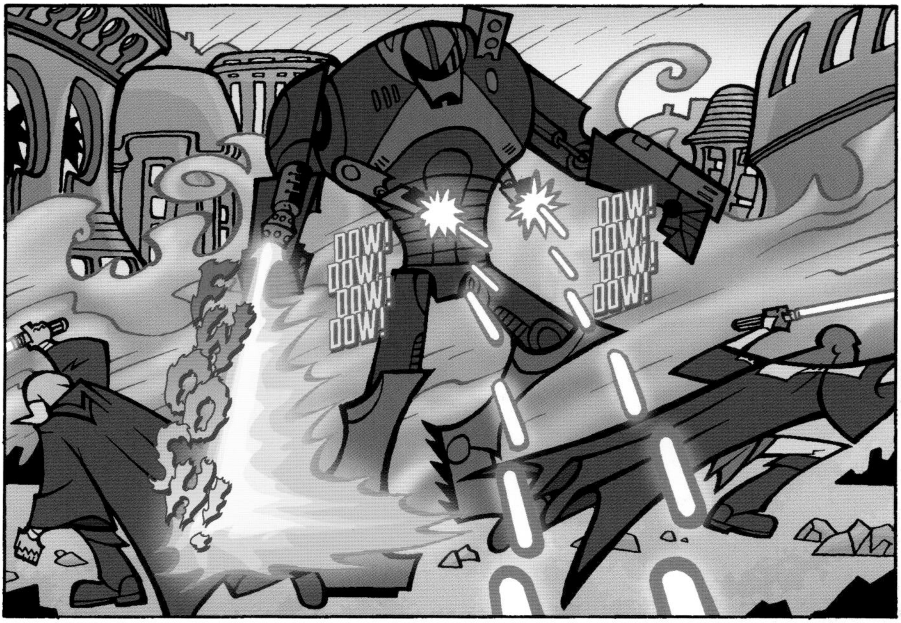
DOW! DOW! DOW! DOW!
DOW! DOW! DOW! DOW!

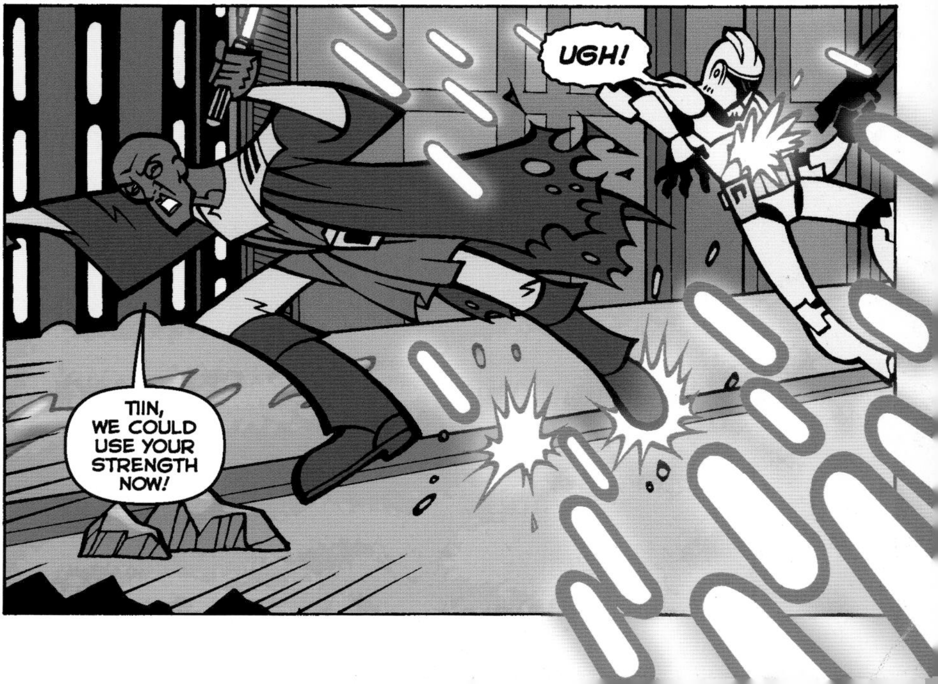
UGH!
TIIN, WE COULD USE YOUR STRENGTH NOW!

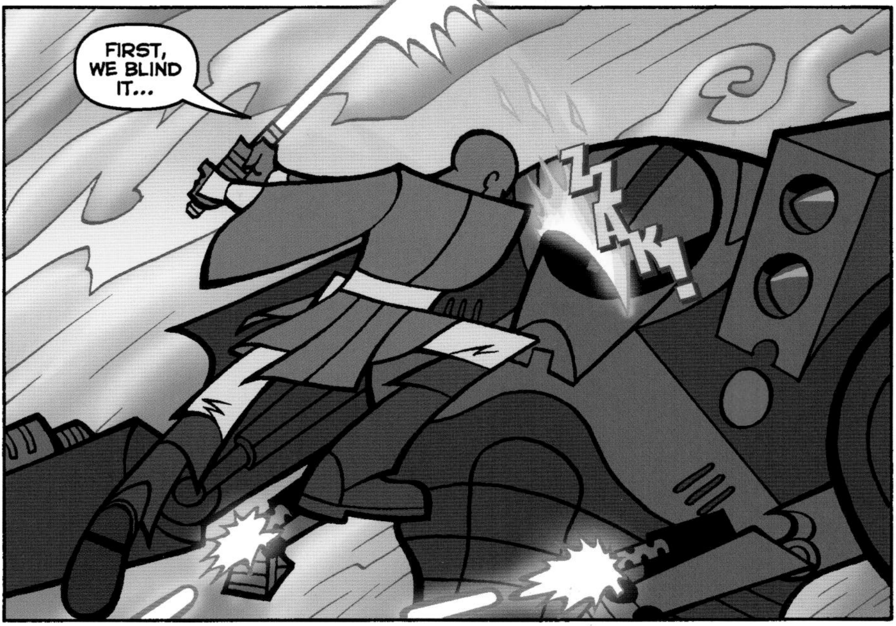
FIRST, WE BLIND IT...
ZZAK!

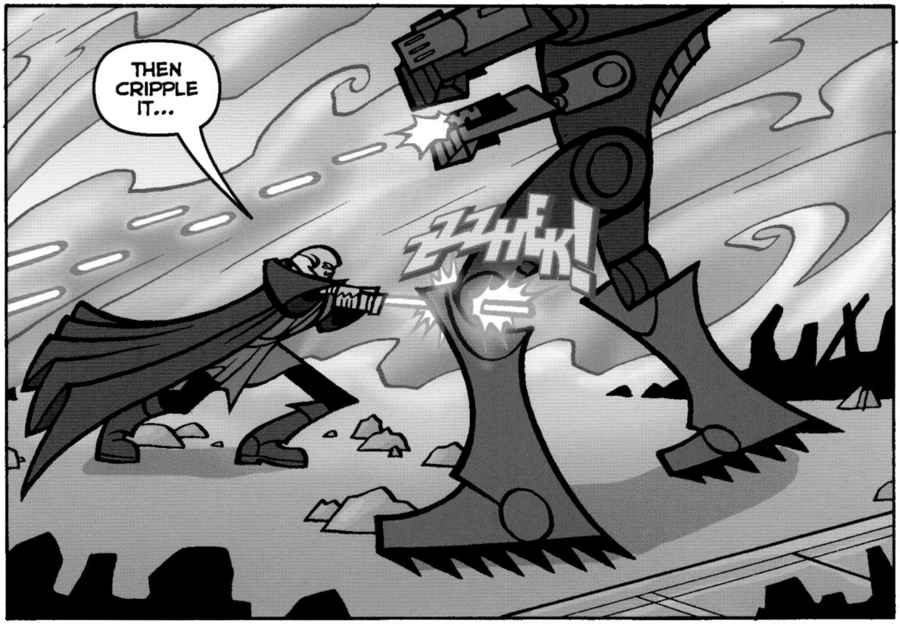
THEN CRIPPLE IT...

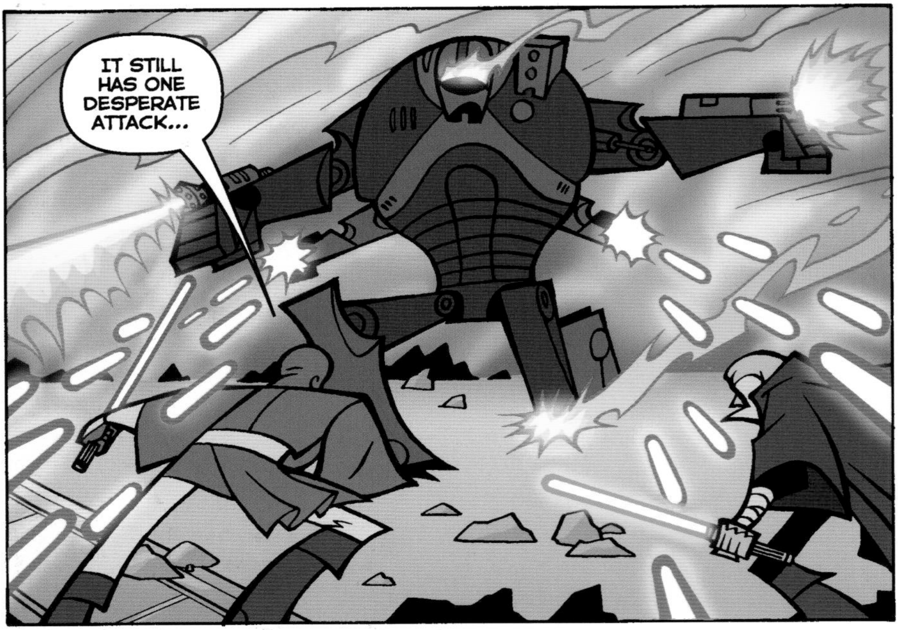
IT STILL HAS ONE DESPERATE ATTACK...

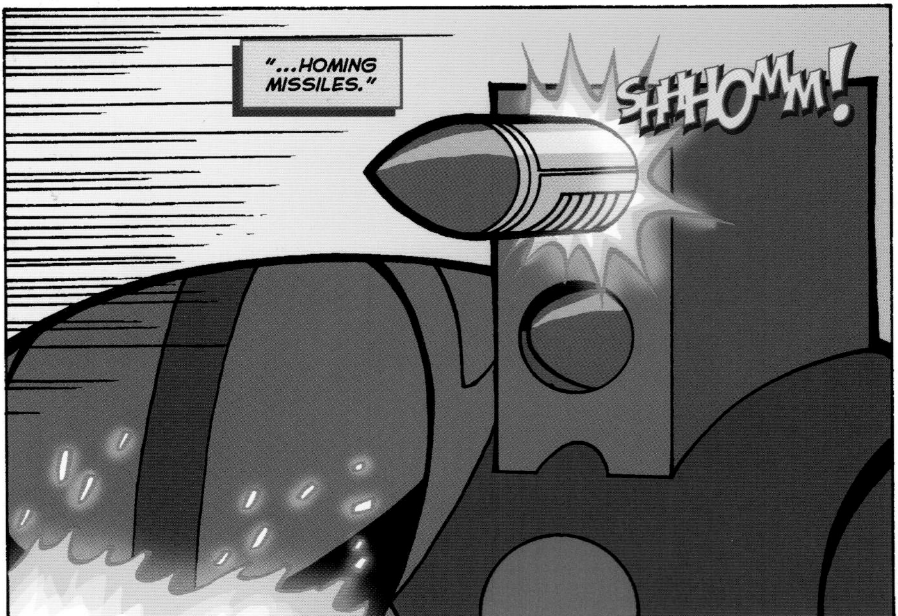
"...HOMING MISSILES."
SHHHOMM!

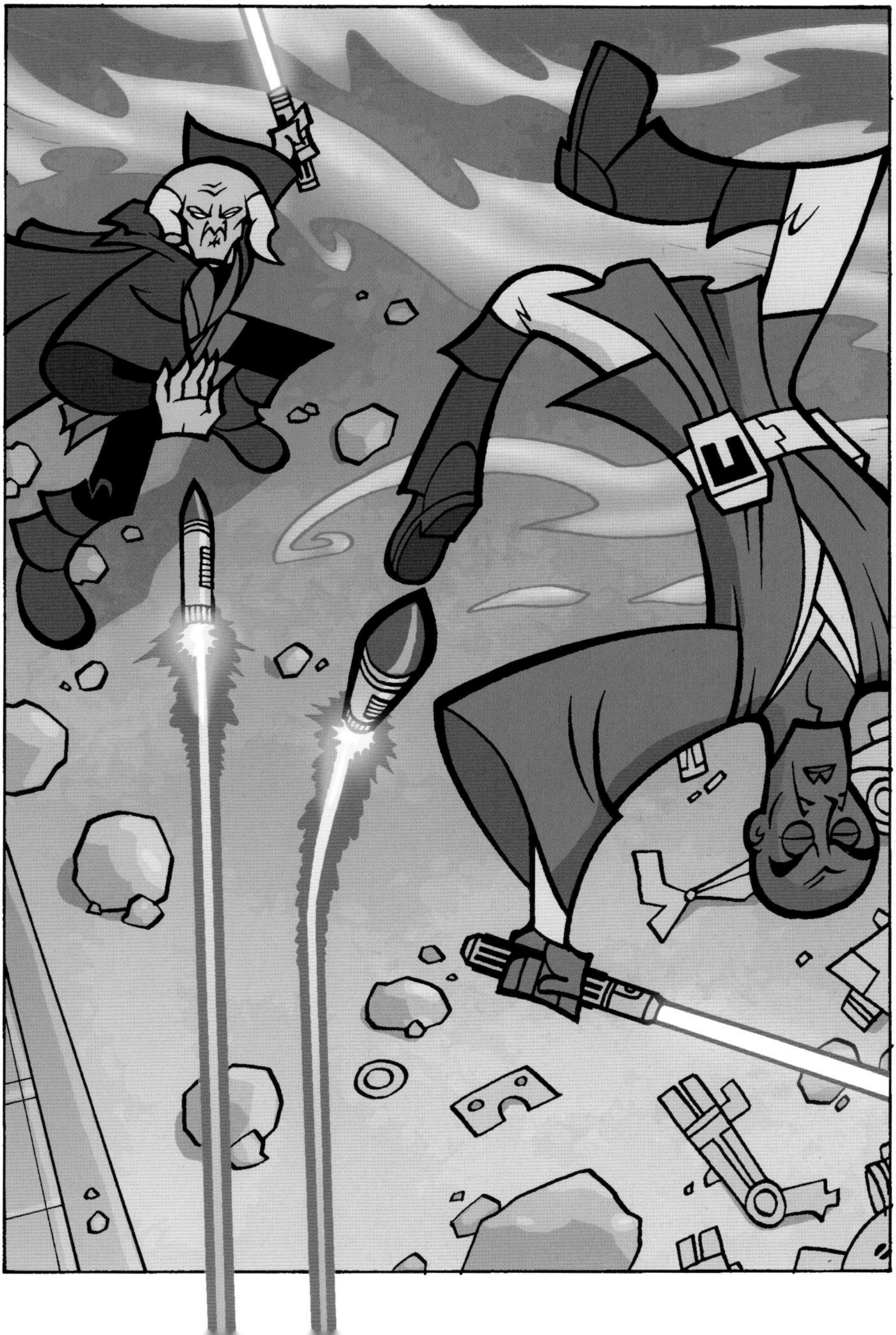

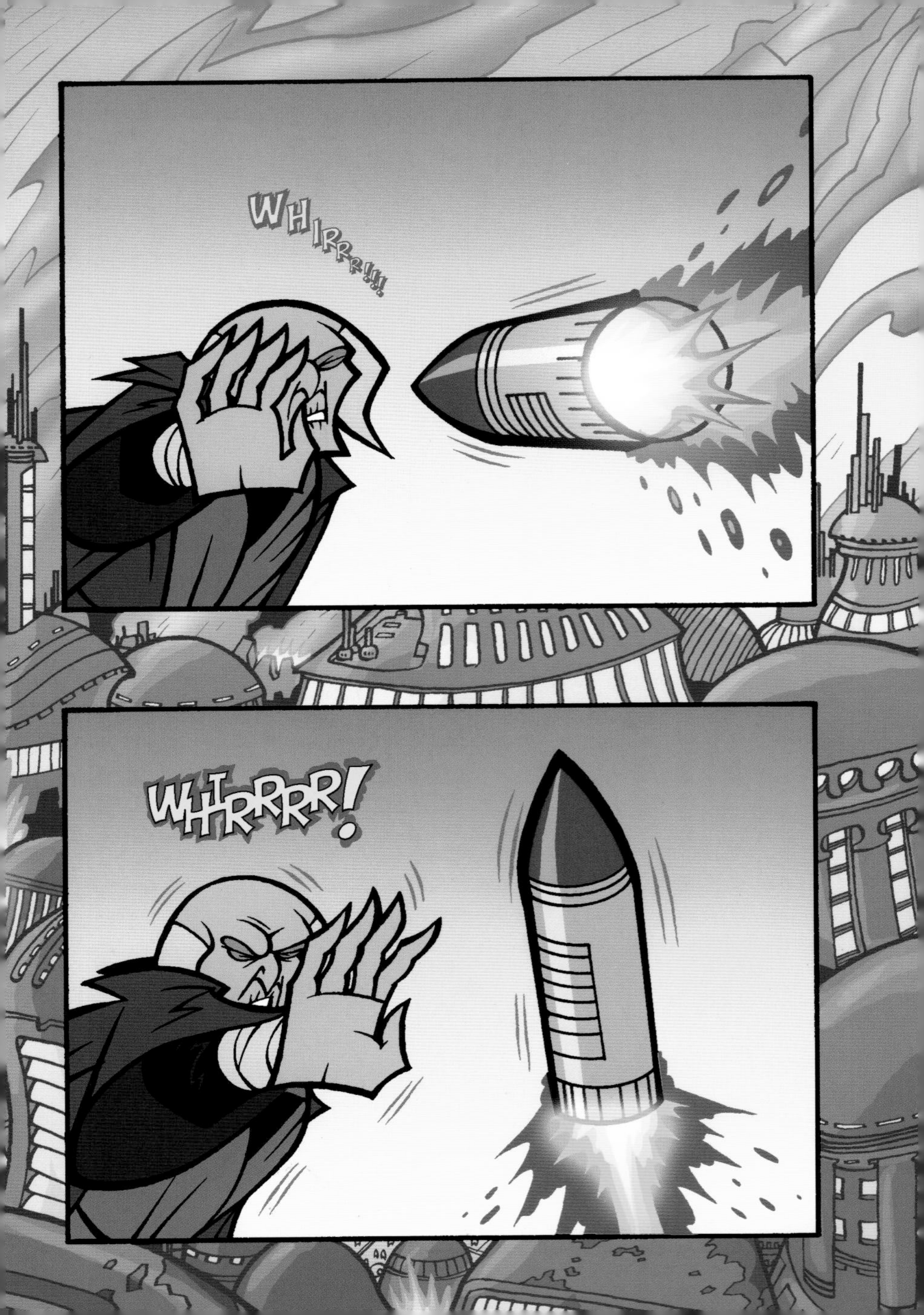
WHIRRR!!!
WHIRRRR!

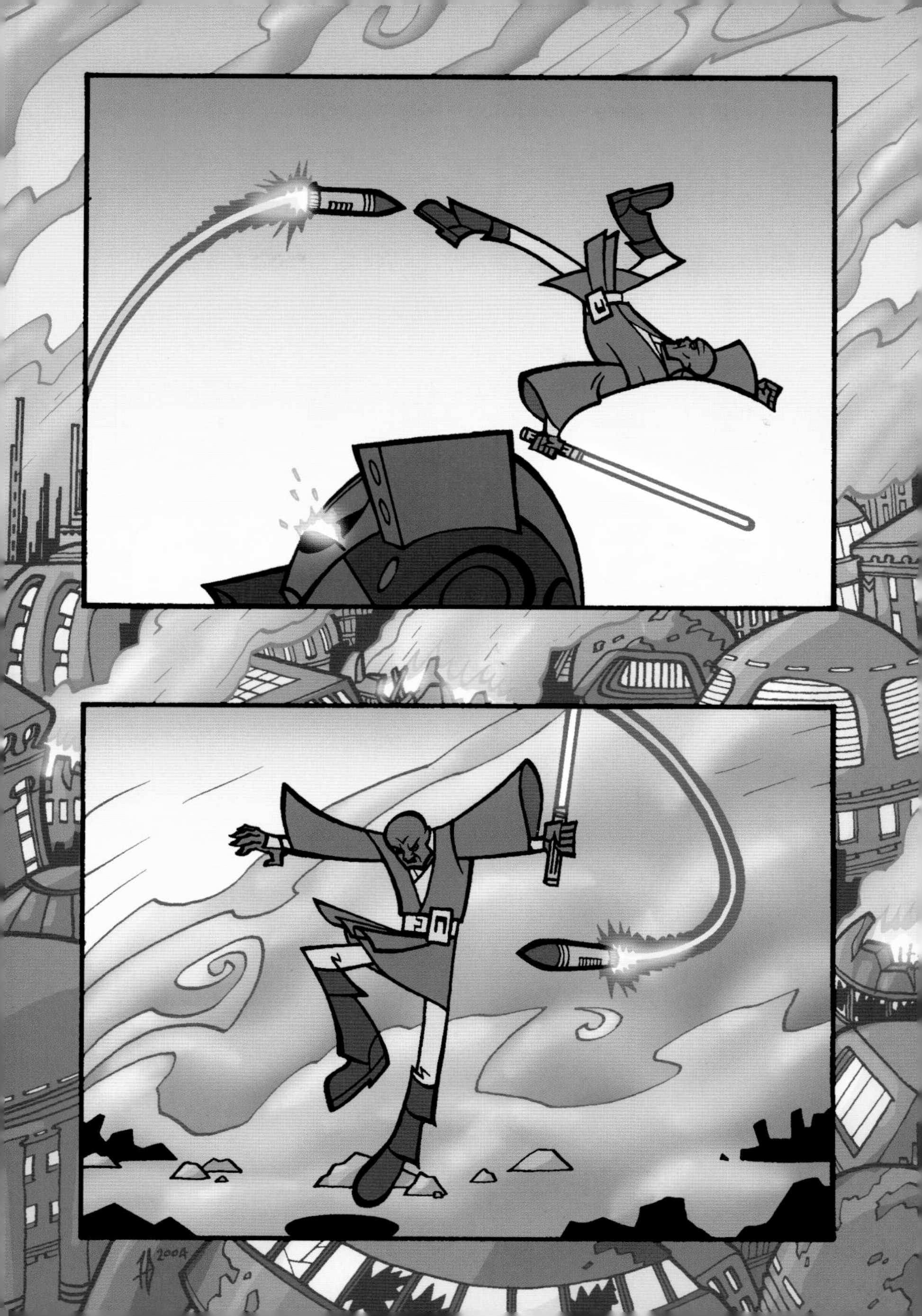

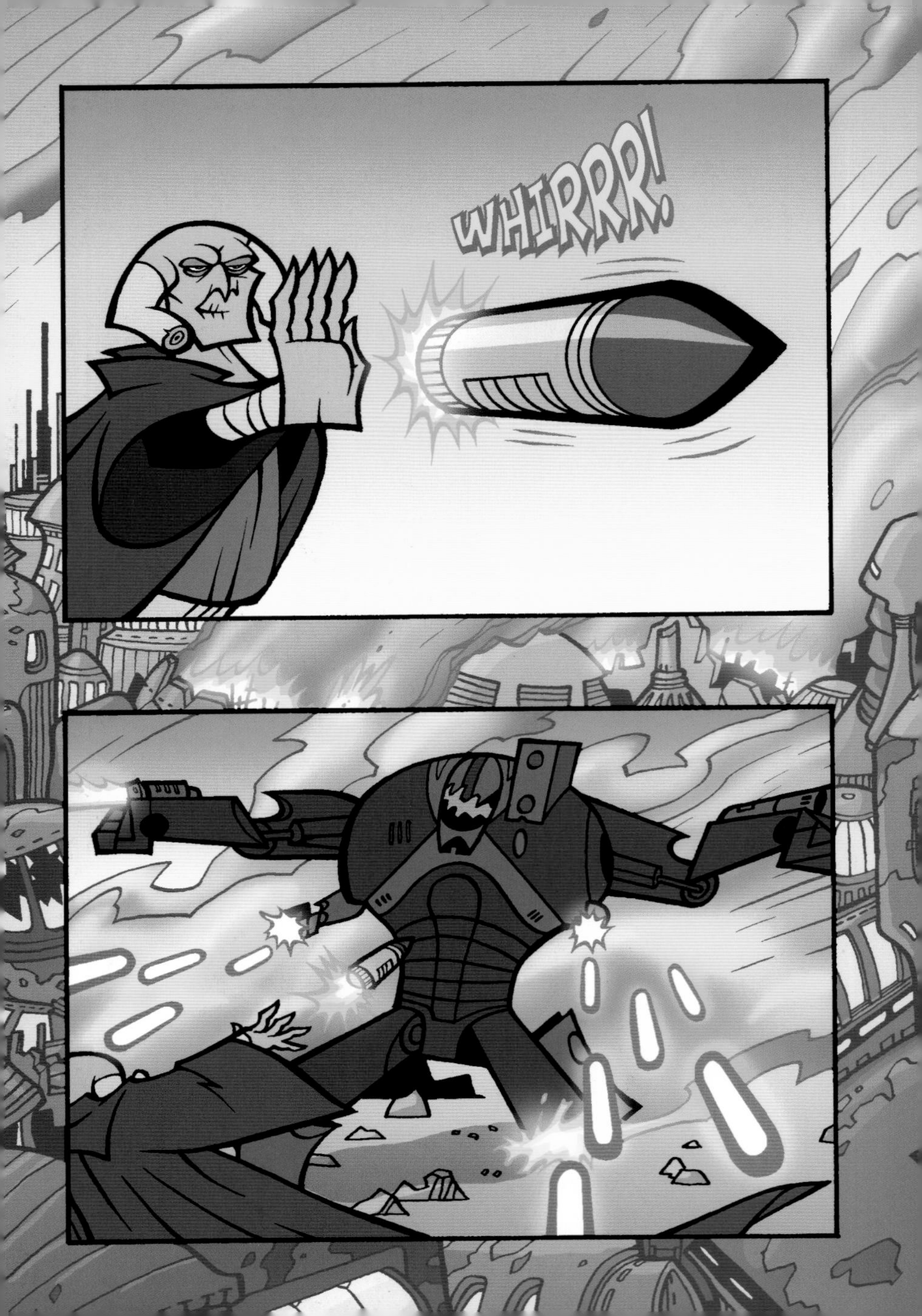
WHIRRR!

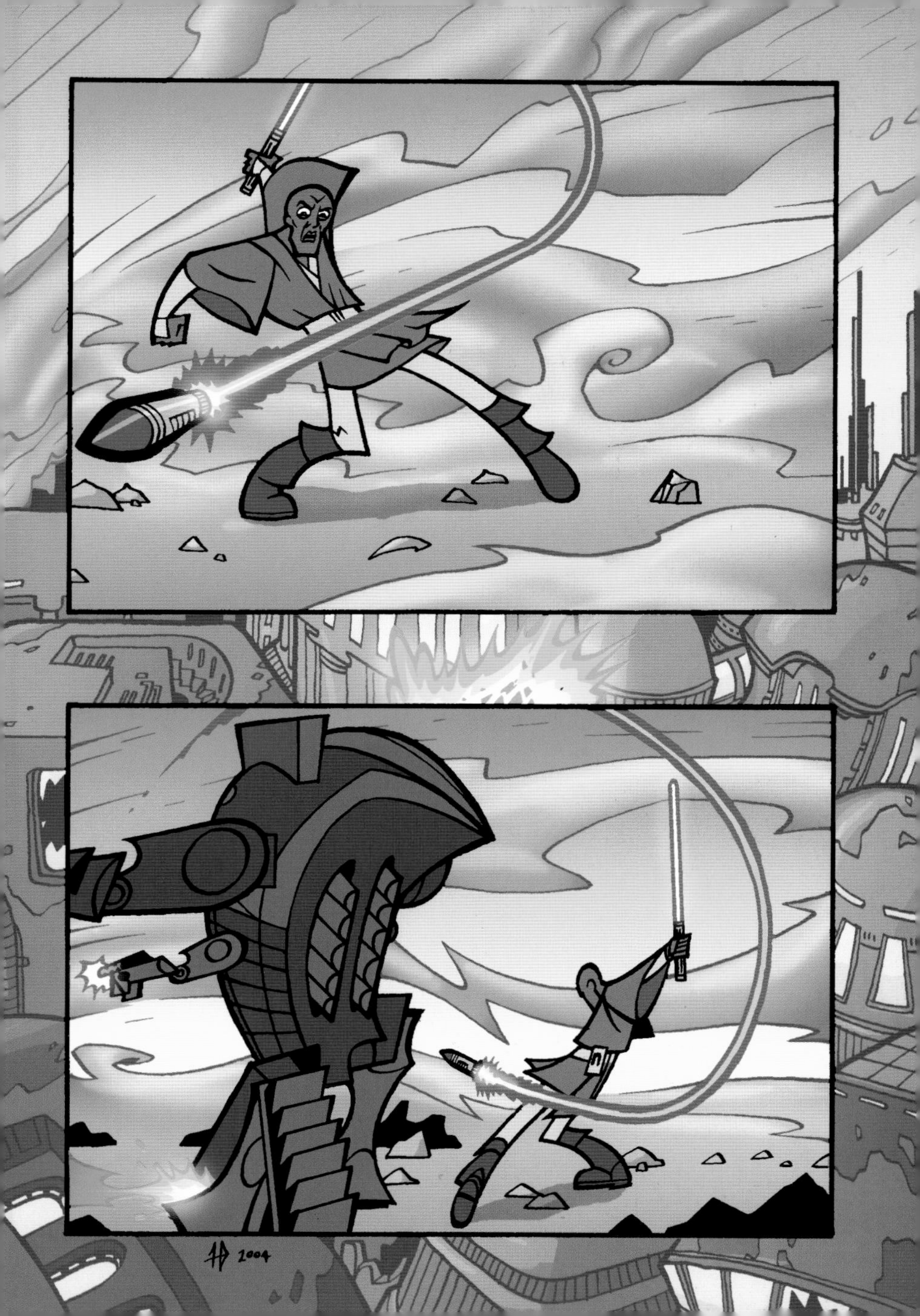
2004

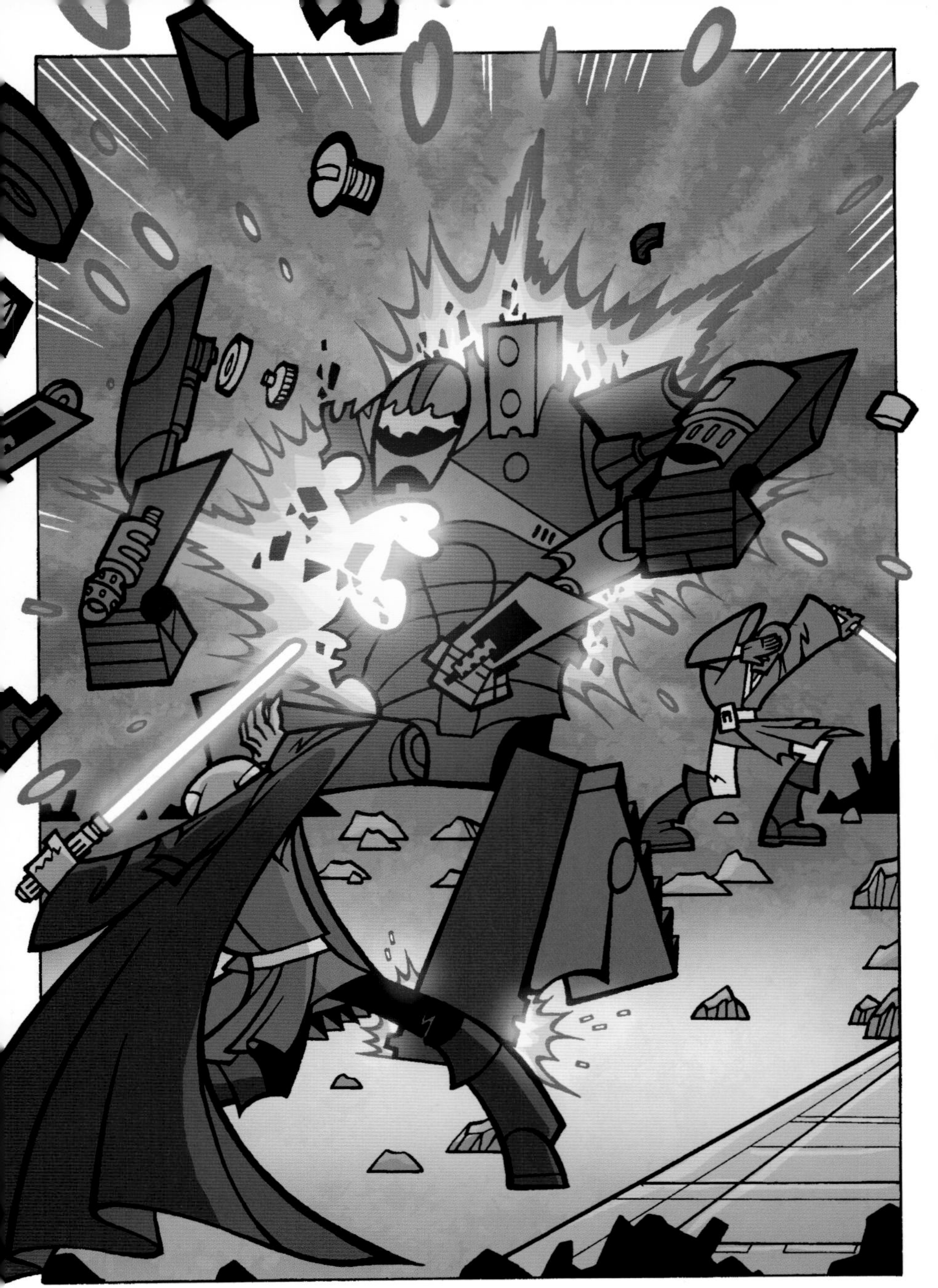

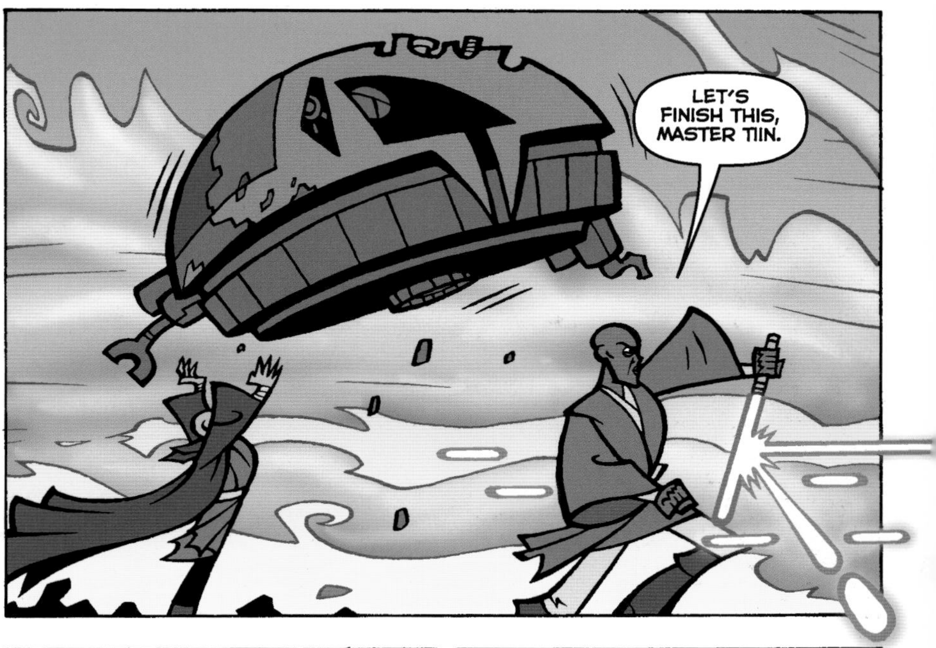
LET'S FINISH THIS, MASTER TIIN.

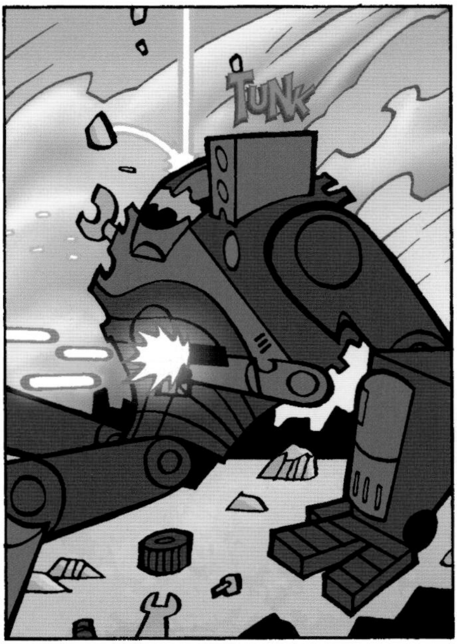
TUNK

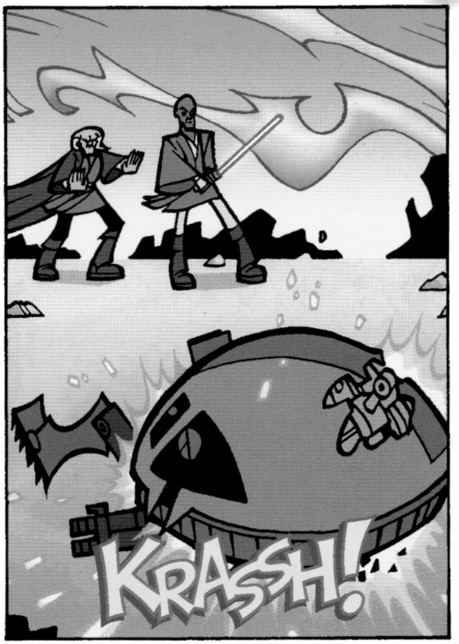
KRASH!

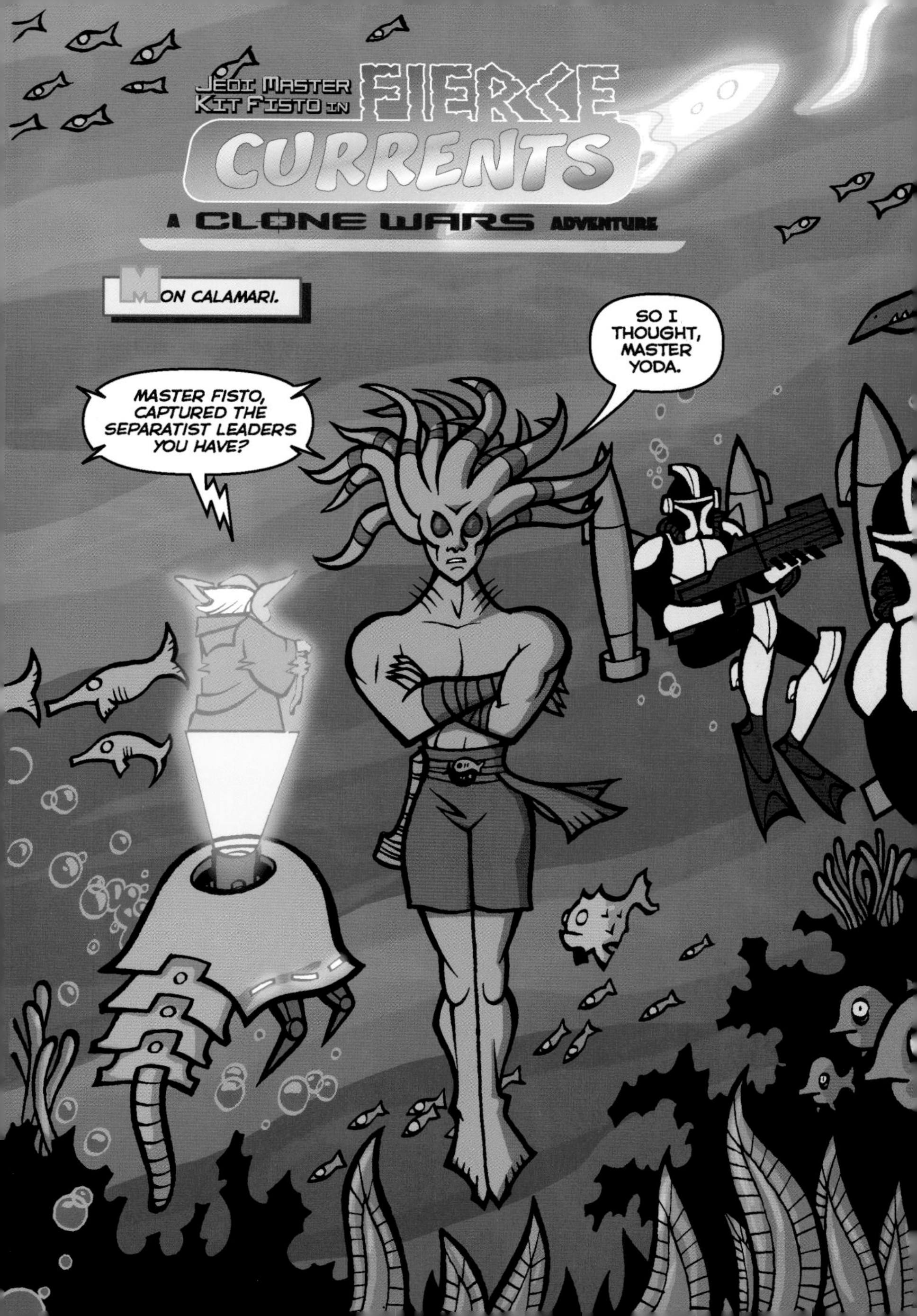
JEDI MASTER KIT FISTO IN
FIERCE CURRENTS
A CLONE WARS ADVENTURE
MON CALAMARI.
MASTER FISTO, CAPTURED THE SEPARATIST LEADERS YOU HAVE?
SO I THOUGHT, MASTER YODA.

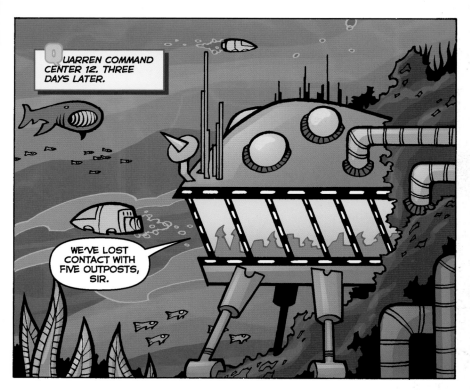

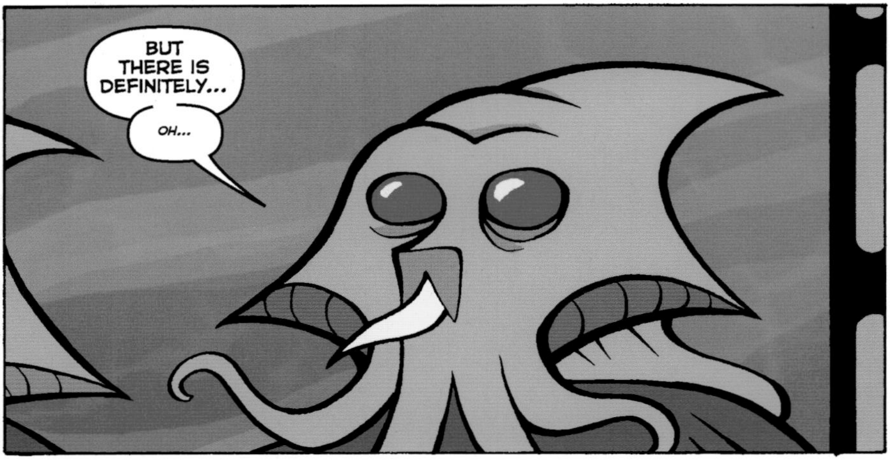
BUT THERE IS DEFINITELY...
OH...

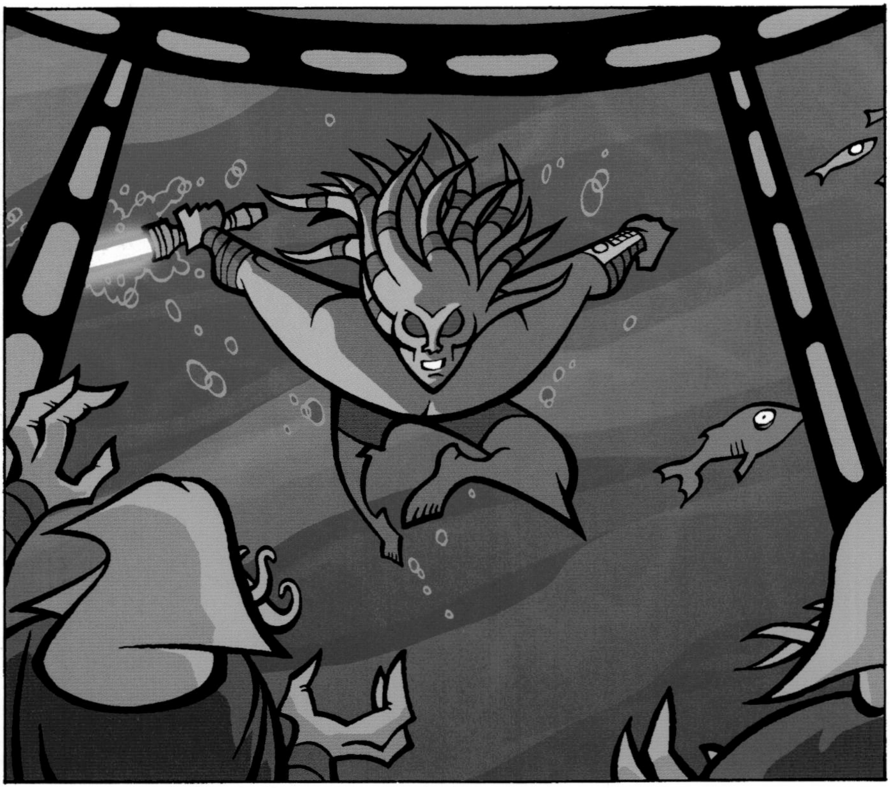

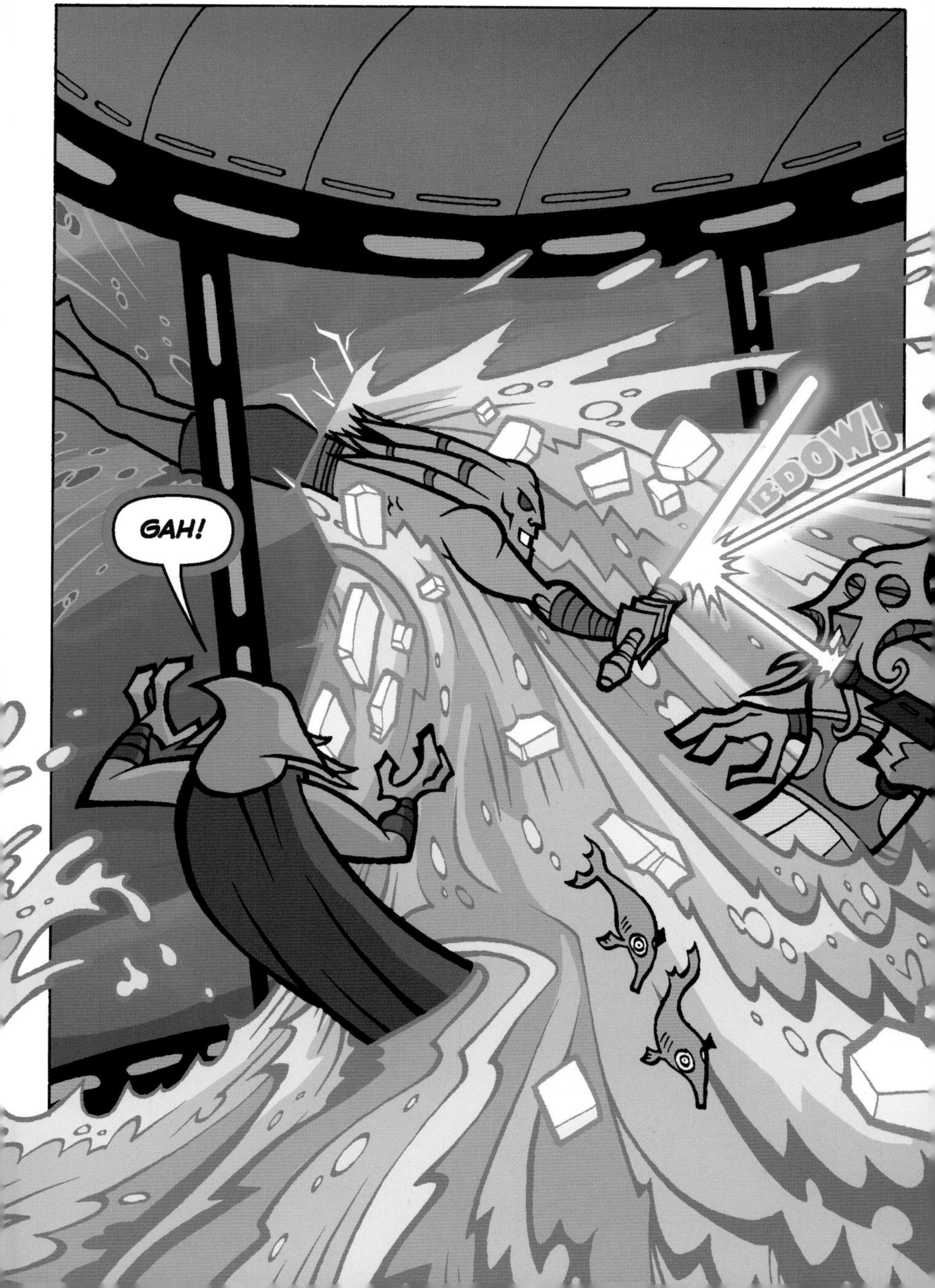
GAH!
BDOW!

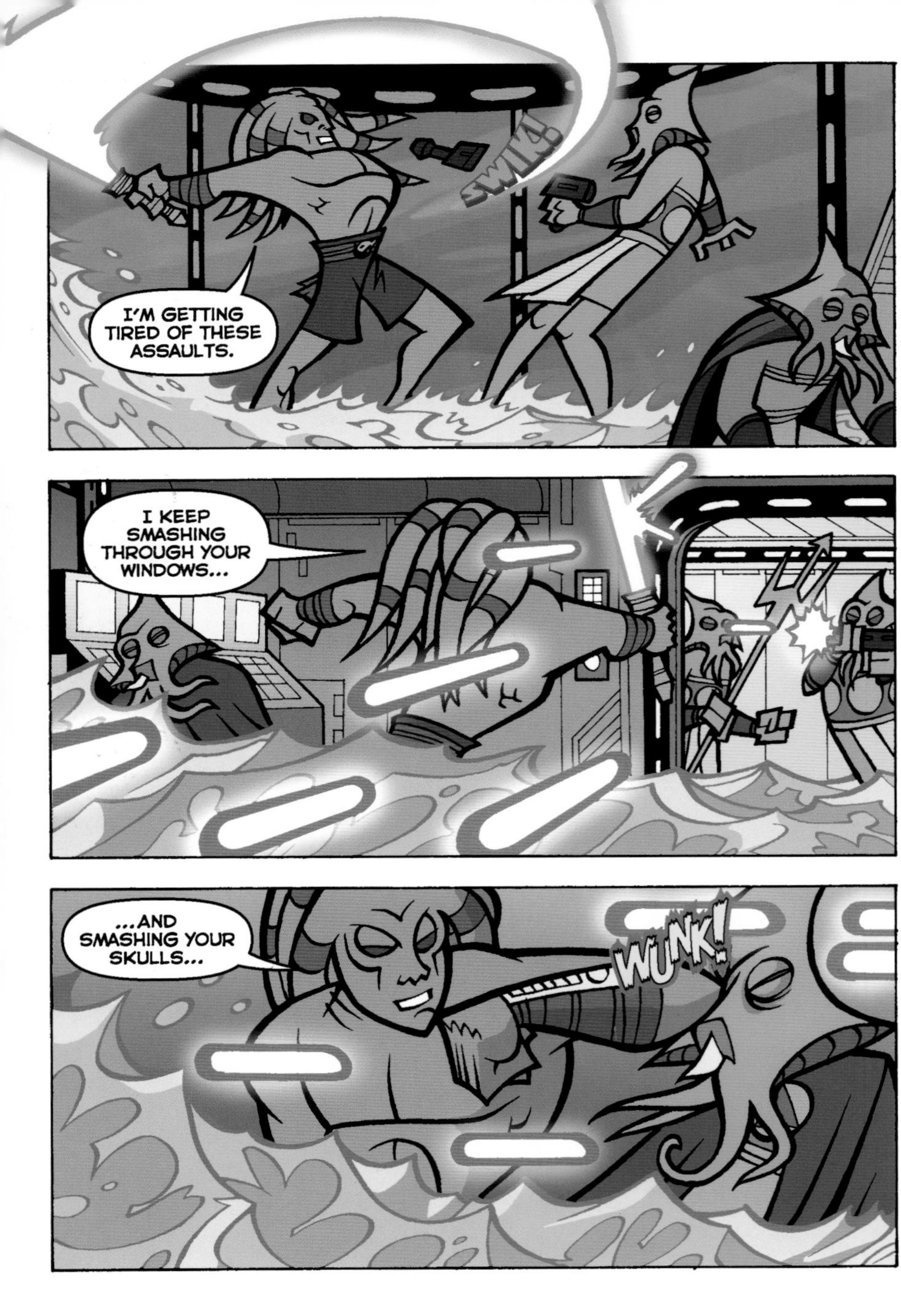
SWIK!
I'M GETTING TIRED OF THESE ASSAULTS.
I KEEP SMASHING THROUGH YOUR WINDOWS...
...AND SMASHING YOUR SKULLS...
WUNK!

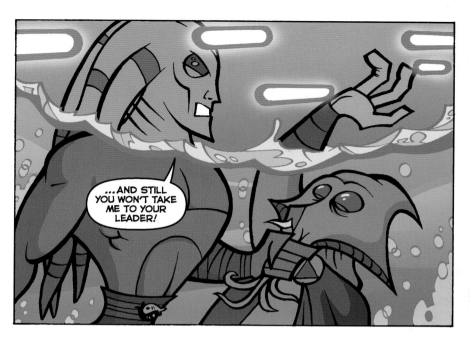

...AND STILL YOU WON'T TAKE ME TO YOUR LEADER!

WE... WE CAN'T! WE DON'T KNOW WHO HE IS!

THEN HOW DO YOU RECEIVE YOUR ORDERS? WHERE DO THEY COME FROM?

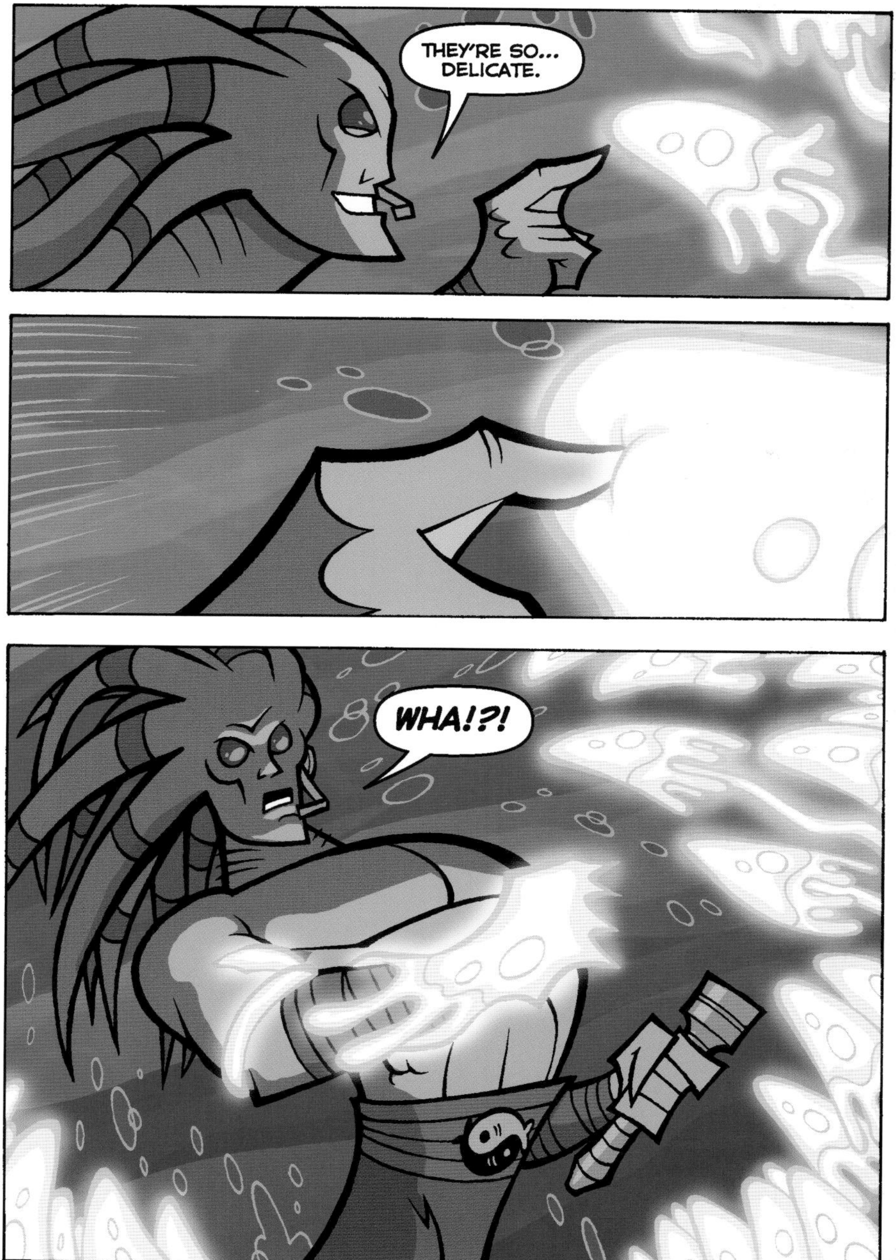
THEY'RE SO... DELICATE.
WHA!?!

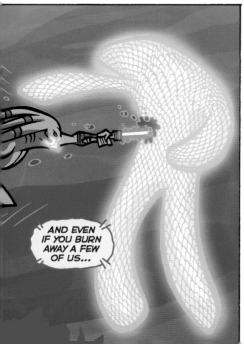

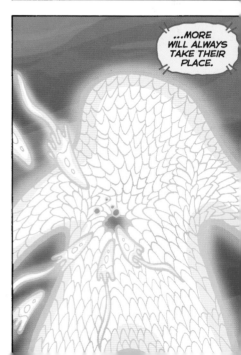

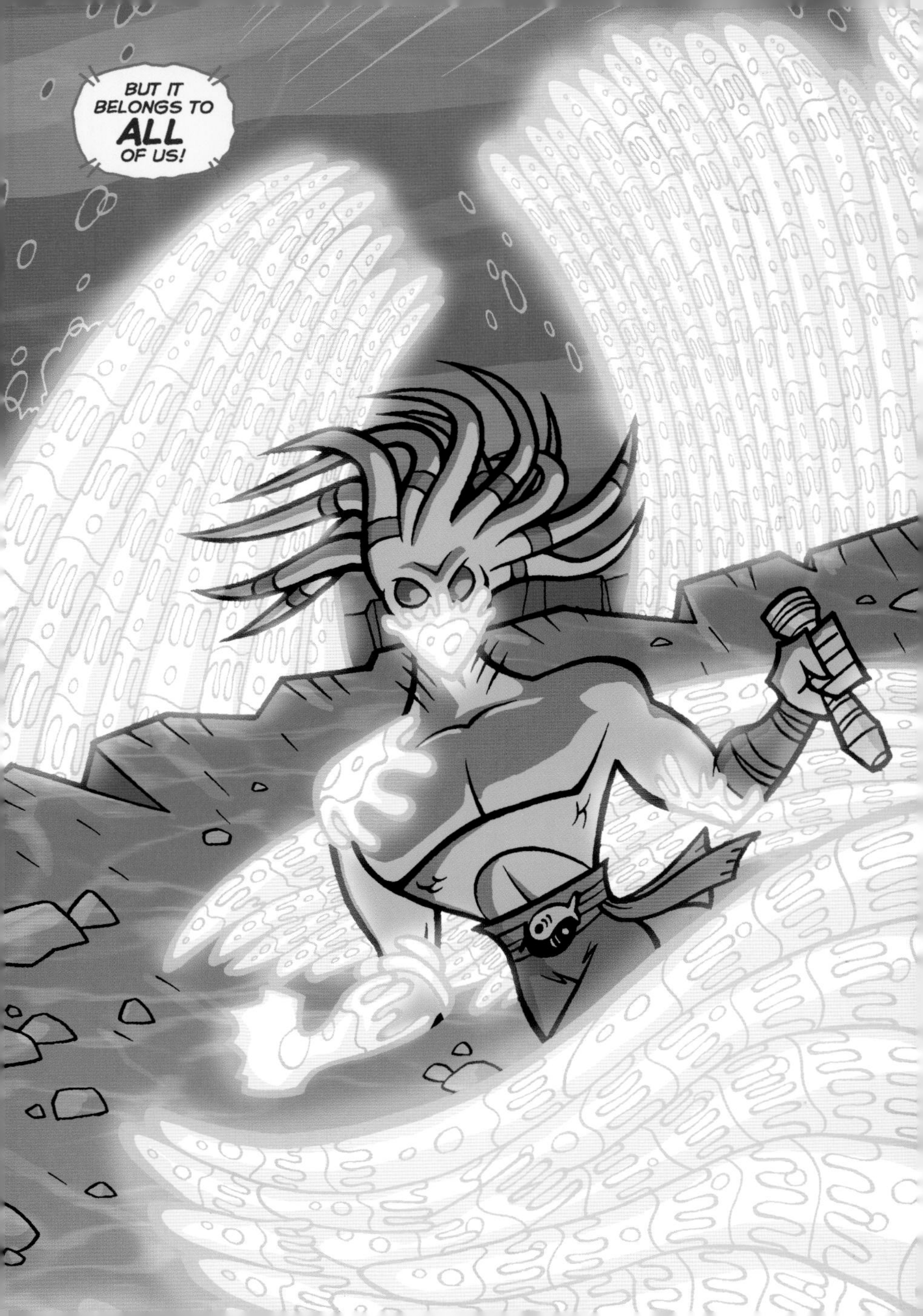
BUT IT BELONGS TO ALL OF US!

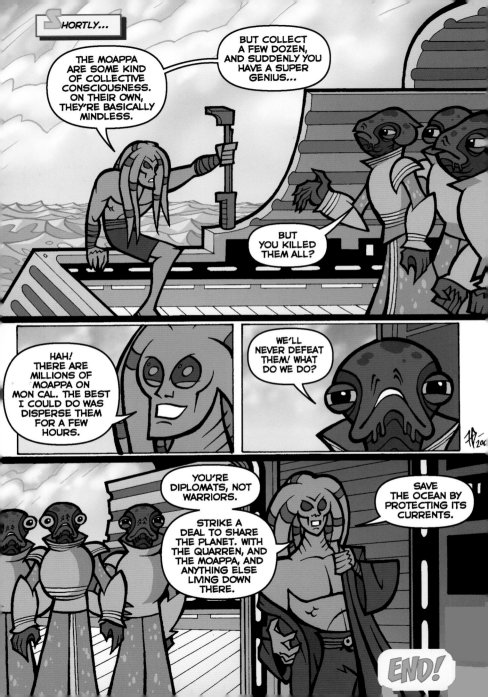

CLONE WARS ADVENTURES

Don't miss any of the action-packed adventures of your favorite **STAR WARS**® characters, availble at comics shops and bookstores in a galaxy near you!

Volume 1
ISBN: 1-59307-243-0 / $6.95

Volume 2
ISBN: 1-59307-271-6 / $6.95

Volume 3
ISBN: 1-59307-307-0 / $6.95

Volume 4
ISBN: 1-59307-402-6 / $6.95

STAR WARS®
CLONE WARS

Experience all the excitement and drama of the Clone Wars! Look for these trade paperbacks at a comics shop or book store near you!

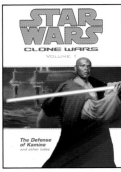

Volume 1
ISBN: 1-56971-962-4 / $14.95

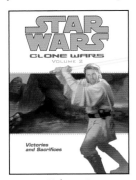

Volume 2
ISBN: 1-56971-969-1 / $14.95

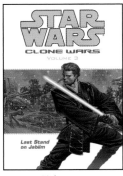

Volume 3
ISBN: 1-59307-006-3 / $14.95

Volume 4
ISBN: 1-59307-195-7 / $16.95

ALSO AVAILABLE

Volume 5
ISBN: 1-59307-273-2 / $14.95

Volume 6
ISBN: 1-59307-352-6 / $17.95

STAR WARS®
TIMELINE OF TRADE PAPERBACKS AND GRAPHIC NOVELS!

OLD REPUBLIC ERA:
25,000-1000 YEARS BEFORE
STAR WARS: A NEW HOPE

Tales of the Jedi—
Knights of the Old Republic
ISBN: 1-56971-020-1 $14.95

Dark Lords of the Sith
ISBN: 1-56971-095-3 $17.95

The Sith War
ISBN: 1-56971-173-9 $17.95

The Golden Age of the Sith
ISBN: 1-56971-229-8 $16.95

The Freedon Nadd Uprising
ISBN: 1-56971-307-3 $5.95

The Fall of the Sith Empire
ISBN: 1-56971-320-0 $15.95

Redemption
ISBN: 1-56971-535-1 $14.95

Jedi vs. Sith
ISBN: 1-56971-649-8 $17.95

RISE OF THE EMPIRE ERA:
1000-0 YEARS BEFORE
STAR WARS: A NEW HOPE

The Stark Hyperspace War
ISBN: 1-56971-985-3 $12.95

Prelude to Rebellion
ISBN: 1-56971-448-7 $14.95

Jedi Council—Acts of War
ISBN: 1-56971-539-4 $12.95

Darth Maul
ISBN: 1-56971-542-4 $12.95

Jedi Council—
Emissaries to Malastare
ISBN: 1-56971-545-9 $15.95

Episode I—
The Phantom Menace
ISBN: 1-56971-359-6 $12.95

Episode I—
The Phantom Menace Adventures
ISBN: 1-56971-443-6 $12.95

Outlander
ISBN: 1-56971-514-9 $14.95

Star Wars: Jango Fett—
Open Seasons
ISBN: 1-56971-671-4 $12.95

The Bounty Hunters
ISBN: 1-56971-467-3 $12.95

Twilight
ISBN: 1-56971-558-0 $12.95

The Hunt for Aurra Sing
ISBN: 1-56971-651-X $12.95

Darkness
ISBN: 1-56971-659-5 $12.95

The Rite of Passage
ISBN: 1-59307-042-X $12.95

Episode II—Attack of the Clones
ISBN: 1-56971-609-9 $17.95

Clone Wars Volume 1:
The Defense of Kamino
ISBN: 1-56971-962-4 $14.95

Clone Wars Volume 2:
Victories and Sacrifices
ISBN: 1-56971-969-1 $14.95

Clone Wars Adventures Volume 1
ISBN: 1-59307-243-0 $6.95

Clone Wars Volume 3:
Last Stand on Jabiim
ISBN: 1-59307-006-3 $14.95

Clone Wars Volume 4: Light and Dark
ISBN: 1-59307-195-7 $16.95

Droids—The Kalarba Adventures
ISBN: 1-56971-064-3 $17.95

Droids—Rebellion
ISBN: 1-56971-224-7 $14.95

Classic Star Wars—
Han Solo At Stars' End
ISBN: 1-56971-254-9 $6.95

Boba Fett—Enemy of The Empire
ISBN: 1-56971-407-X $12.95

Dark Forces—
Soldier for the Empire GSA
ISBN: 1-56971-348-0 $14.95

Mara Jade—By the Emperor's Hand
ISBN: 1-56971-401-0 $15.95

Underworld
ISBN: 1-56971-618-8 $15.95

Empire Volume 1: Betrayal
ISBN: 1-56971-964-0 $12.95

Empire Volume 2: Darklighter
ISBN: 1-56971-975-6 $17.95

REBELLION ERA:
0-5 YEARS AFTER
STAR WARS: A NEW HOPE

Classic Star Wars, Volume 1:
In Deadly Pursuit
ISBN: 1-56971-109-7 $16.95

Classic Star Wars, Volume 2:
The Rebel Storm
ISBN: 1-56971-106-2 $16.95

Classic Star Wars, Volume 3:
Escape to Hoth
ISBN: 1-56971-093-7 $16.95

Classic Star Wars—
The Early Adventures
ISBN: 1-56971-178-X $19.95

Jabba the Hutt—The Art of the Deal
ISBN: 1-56971-310-3 $9.95

Vader's Quest
ISBN: 1-56971-415-0 $11.95

Splinter of the Mind's Eye
ISBN: 1-56971-223-9 $14.95

A Long Time Ago... Volume 1:
Doomworld
ISBN: 1-56971-754-0 $29.95

A Long Time Ago... Volume 2:
Dark Encounters
ISBN: 1-56971-785-0 $29.95

A Long Time Ago... Volume 3:
Resurrection of Evil
ISBN: 1-56971-786-9 $29.95

A Long Time Ago... Volume 4:
Screams in the Void
ISBN: 1-56971-787-7 $29.95

A Long Time Ago... Volume 5:
Fool's Bounty
ISBN: 1-56971-906-3 $29.95

A Long Time Ago... Volume 6:
Wookiee World
ISBN: 1-56971-907-1 $29.95

A Long Time Ago... Volume 7:
Far, Far Away
ISBN: 1-56971-908-X $29.95

Battle of the Bounty Hunters
Pop-Up Book
ISBN: 1-56971-129-1 $17.95

Shadows of the Empire
ISBN: 1-56971-183-6 $17.95

The Empire Strikes Back—
The Special Edition
ISBN: 1-56971-234-4 $9.95

Return of the Jedi—The Special Edition
ISBN: 1-56971-235-2 $9.95

NEW REPUBLIC ERA:
5-25 YEARS AFTER
STAR WARS: A NEW HOPE

X-Wing Rouge Squadron
The Phantom Affair
ISBN: 1-56971-251-4 $12.95

Battleground Tatooine
ISBN: 1-56971-276-X $12.95

The Warrior Princess
ISBN: 1-56971-330-8 $12.95

Requiem for a Rogue
ISBN: 1-56971-331-6 $12.95

In the Empire's Service
ISBN: 1-56971-383-9 $12.95

Blood and Honor
ISBN: 1-56971-387-1 $12.95

Masquerade
ISBN: 1-56971-487-8 $12.95

Mandatory Retirement
ISBN: 1-56971-492-4 $12.95

Shadows of the Empire
Evolution
ISBN: 1-56971-441-X $14.95

Heir to the Empire
ISBN: 1-56971-202-6 $19.95

Dark Force Rising
ISBN: 1-56971-269-7 $17.95

The Last Command
ISBN: 1-56971-378-2 $17.95

Dark Empire
ISBN: 1-59307-039-X $16.95

Dark Empire II
ISBN: 1-56971-119-4 $17.95

Empire's End
ISBN: 1-56971-306-5 $5.95

Boba Fett—Death, Lies, & Treachery
ISBN: 1-56971-311-1 $12.95

Crimson Empire
ISBN: 1-56971-355-3 $17.95

Crimson Empire II—Council of Blood
ISBN: 1-56971-410-X $17.95

Jedi Academy—Leviathan
ISBN: 1-56971-456-8 $11.95

Union
ISBN: 1-56971-464-9 $12.95

NEW JEDI ORDER ERA:
25+ YEARS AFTER
STAR WARS: A NEW HOPE

Chewbacca
ISBN: 1-56971-515-7 $12.95

INFINITIES:
DOES NOT APPLY TO TIMELINE

Infinities — A New Hope
ISBN: 1-56971-648-X $12.95

Infinities—The Empire Strikes Back
ISBN: 1-56971-904-7 $12.95

Infinities—Return of the Jedi
ISBN: 1-59307-206-6 $12.95

Star Wars Tales Volume 1
ISBN: 1-56971-619-6 $19.95

Star Wars Tales Volume 2
ISBN: 1-56971-757-5 $19.95

Star Wars Tales Volume 3
ISBN: 1-56971-836-9 $19.95

Star Wars Tales Volume 4
ISBN: 1-56971-989-6 $19.95

AVAILABLE AT YOUR LOCAL COMICS SHOP OR BOOKSTORE
To find a comics shop in your area, call 1-888-266-4226
For more information or to order direct: • On the web: www.darkhorse.com • E-mail: mailorder@darkhorse.com
• Phone: 1-800-862-0052 or (503) 652-9701 Mon.-Sat. 9 A.M. to 5 P.M. Pacific Time